WRITE
BIG

VICTORIA PAYNE

To the belief in love at first sight...
To my sons, Chaz, Dezi, and Nico—
I was yours the moment we met.

CONTENTS

"If we had to say what writing is,
we would define it essentially as an act of courage."
— Cythia Ozick

THE COLLEGE APPLICATION ESSAY AS WRITING CLASS

The world of college awaits.

But first the college visits, the applications, the essays. It's tempting to see the process as a series of steps to complete before you can start your real life, but I invite you to see this time in your life not as a temporary weigh station but as an integral part of your story. In fact, this time in your life is one of the many experiences that will shape you as a person, as you move into making perhaps the first independent decision of your life.

It's this little shift, this subtle reimagining, that helps you grasp the first lesson I want to teach you about writing your college application essay—writing is not separate from all the other elements that accompany your application, it's not some activity you'll perform in addition to calculations of GPA and test scores, reviews of teacher recommendations, and lists of accomplishments. The college application essay is the narration of your story—it's your way of explaining how the data points of your life add up and what they mean.

But that's why we don't like it, Victoria! I didn't say it was going to be easy, but neither is college. And that's where you want to go, right? I believe the challenge of writing your college application essay is an ideal way to introduce you to two important requirements college demands:

1. Intellectual inquiry
2. Strong Writing Skills.

Embrace the Transformation

Recently, I had a conversation with a fellow educator who works with college-bound seniors. She lamented the poor quality of students' writing and her belief that without editing their work, they could never manage to gain acceptance into college on their own.

At the time of our conversation, I was in the middle of writing this book, a book I want in the hands of every college-bound senior writing a college application essay, a book I believe can guide them to better writing. I wondered at the sentiment that students need someone to *fix* their writing, so they can attend a college that will demand abilities they seemingly do not have. How will this work out for them?

In some ways, I already knew. With almost twenty years of experience teaching writing to college freshmen and upperclassmen, I know the quality of most undergrads' writing. Unlike my colleague, I do not see them as hopeless, but untrained. I truly love helping students discover good ideas and showing them how to translate them into beautiful prose. From new students transitioning to college and learning the demands of college writing, to students graduating and heading for medical school, my goal has always been to transform students into writers.

Turning students into writers is the philosophy that underlies this book. In it, I am giving you my experience from years of coaching students to craft remarkable admissions essays. But I am also giving you the benefit of my years of teaching composition and personal narrative writing in the university classroom. In other words, I believe the process outlined throughout this book and the act of creating a college application essay will actually advance your writing skills *before* college. While the genre of the college application essay is a mutant form—half story, half analytical essay, all for admissions readers—many of the skills within these chapters translate to how to think and write for any audience.

How to Use This Book

This book has it all. Everything you need to create your own college application essay masterpiece.

Perhaps the most useful part of this book was not written by me, but your fellow college-bound seniors. If you don't read anything else in this book, I highly recommend reading these essays as a starting point. Together they showcase the storytelling approach I've been teaching students for years. And they are models of inspiration.

The book is designed as a how-to guide for writing a knockout college application essay but also *how to write in general*. This lesson is something I know many students need because it's something I do in my private coaching practice—helping students translate ideas into language, creating great introductions, constructing strong paragraphs, and so forth. Part I introduces you to the storytelling mindset and will help you select a winning topic.

Part II builds on the formula introduced in part I and explains the key ingredients that go into each paragraph of the college application essay in order to write remarkably in 650 words or less. The final chapter of part II provides advanced instruction on next-level writing and is a must for anyone who wants to wow the admission counselor. You'll find the sample essays in part III of the book.

I highly recommend reading all of the chapters—I wrote them for you. I believe it's reasonable for you to move through these chapters in a week or two by focusing on a chapter or two per day. If you love the storytelling approach introduced in these chapters but want personal coaching and accountability, check out the online workshops that are a perfect companion to *Write Big*. You can find workshop information and free resources created to accompany this book at writebig.net/resources.

It's hard to condense twenty years of teaching and coaching writers into one book, much less my passion for mentoring young people. My best attempt at solving this problem was to create a section at the end of each chapter called a "Bachelors in Brainwork." This title speaks to my belief that the college experience is more than an education but also a journey designed for emotional and intellectual transformation. The content in these sections leads you to think deeply about not only the process of writing a college application essay for an admissions audience but *how* you'll navigate the experience of college life and *what* you'll do with the time after you receive admission into college. To help you answer these questions, I created an online guide with articles and resources to accompany *Write Big*. Sign up to receive access to all of these great materials at writebig.net/resources.

What Not To Do

In my college classes, I like to help my students understand the way academia views plagiarism. I give them this analogy: In high school copying someone's ideas or words is sort of like lying—you know you shouldn't do it, but you might do it anyway. In college, however, plagiarism is like murder—it's crossing a line of no return.

If you are feeling nervous about applying to college and tempted to borrow an essay from this book I want you to consider you might not be ready for college. The students who wrote the essays here spent hours of their lives writing their own stories in order to open doors to their top choice schools. They were rewarded for their authenticity. Are you ready to be yourself? College will demand more of you than your own words.

Also, I believe in you. I wrote this book so you can become a better writer as you apply for college. In chapter 8, Designer Essays, I break down three remarkable essays and show you how they did it. I deconstruct the essay-writing process so you can design your essay from a template you know works. But it must be your ideas, it must be your story, it must be your words.

Finally, I'll be sending colleges a note this book has been published with student essays, and in time, many colleges will become familiar with the standouts published here.

Creating an original essay isn't just about avoiding plagiarism, but it's about signing up for a personal journey at a time in your life when self-knowledge is at a premium.

I wish you a bon voyage.

FREQUENTLY ASKED QUESTIONS

What is a college application essay?

A college application essay is the name for the longer essay, generally between 500–650 words, many colleges and universities require as part of your application. The college application essay offers students an opportunity to talk about their lives in meaningful ways or show another side to their identity not captured by GPA, test scores, accomplishments, or activities.

Occasionally, students can choose any topic for the college application essay. If that's the case, I recommend using one of the prompts from the Common Application as a guide.

What is the Common Application?

Many private colleges, public universities, and religious and secular institutions, use the Common Application, a not-for-profit membership organization that provides a streamlined application process in partnership with hundreds of universities. Think of the Common Application as a membership website bringing together college-bound students with universities and colleges to make the application process easier. Note: not every school uses the Common Application.

In addition to important application questions, personal information, and portals for teacher recommendations and other supporting documents, the Common Application contains prompts for essays, with a word count restriction of 650 words or less. These prompts are typically personal and give students pathways for thinking about their lives as identity stories, turning point experiences, and coming-of-age narratives.

How will I know if my school takes the Common Application?

If you create an account on the Common Application, you can input the names of schools where you'll be applying. If your school accepts the Common Application, the college will appear in their database. To create an account, visit the Common Application website at http://www.commonapp.org.

What are the prompts for the Common Application?

The Common Application updates their prompts periodically, so it's best to check their website for yourself: http://www.commonapp.org. Make sure you're always looking at the prompts for the current year, as a quick google search may not provide you with the most recent results. I also have a link to the current Common Application prompts on my website, which I update regularly: www.boxcarwritinglabs.com.

Are there bad prompts for the Common Application essay?

In my experience, almost any prompt on the Common Application can make a great essay. But your approach, the subject of the first part of *Write Big*, is a very important part of the final outcome.

However, I do have some words of caution for two of the prompts.

If you choose to write about "a challenge, setback, or failure," be sure not only to show the lessons you've learned from the experience but also the process you use today to avoid or work through tough problems with similar themes. Colleges would love to see how you've overcome circumstances, but they also want to see you are ready and able for the rigors of their institution. Personally, I like writing about "failure with a twist," meaning it's more interesting when students write about overcoming perfectionism or *failing* to build a 1,000-piece lego ship because of a missing brick. Both of these examples show a mindset of advancement and achievement and foreshadow learning how to become a more emotionally-balanced individual or creative problem solver. For a great essay on failure, see Makenna's "The Upside of Failure" in part III, chapter 15.

Recently, the Common Application added a new prompt. This option asks students to "share a piece of writing from school." As a writing coach, my first thought is *don't fall for that prompt*. Why? Most institutions want you to demonstrate you're a hard worker, willing to take on the challenge of college. I'm not sure submitting an old essay does that. Moreover, the context for creating the original writing is very different from the expectations of the college application essay, so you really can't just slide another essay in and satisfy the "get-to-know-you" opportunity the college application essay provides. You certainly do not want to submit something that wreaks of an assignment; if you need to be enrolled in AP Literature, for example, to understand the idiosyncrasies of the essay, then it's not a good fit. If you do choose this option, I highly recommend extensive revisions to adapt the essay to one of the other prompts. When you submit it as part of your Common Application, select one of the other prompts in conjunction with your essay.

What is the Coalition Application?

The Coalition Application was founded in 2015 and is a universal application system created to support lower-income, first-generation, and under-resourced students. The Coalition Application wants to help these students, often at a disadvantage in the application process and in adjusting to college, to succeed in their undergraduate education and beyond. In addition to providing its own application system, the Coalition Application is a tremendous resource for underserved students. Not every college accepts the Coalition Application, but its list will certainly grow as more universities embrace their vision. You can find their list of partners at their website (see below). Note: The required essay for the Coalition Application is slightly shorter (500-550 words) and the prompts are similar to the Common Application. You can see the prompts at their website at http://coalitionforcollegeaccess.org.

Like the Common Application prompts, be sure to use caution when writing about failure, obstacles, or challenges. Consider devoting half of your essay to describing the process of how you solved this important life problem. Also, for the free choice prompt, if you choose to recycle an old paper (not recommended), follow the guidelines within the chapters of *Write Big* to remodel your work into a standout essay.

I believe *Write Big* is an excellent resource for all college bound students, but I am especially excited to have created a low-cost tool financially accessible to everyone, in addition to many other free resources designed to enhance your learning in *Write Big*.

What are writing supplements for my college application?

There's a huge range of expectations from universities and colleges on how much writing they require from you. *Write Big* is devoted to the longer college application essay, but as you start your college application it's useful to have an understanding of the expectations for these shorter essays.

If you are applying to a state school, you may be asked for very little or no writing. For example, Oregon State University asks for something called an *insight resume*, which is essentially a list of essay questions. The answers are typically 250 words or less.

However, if you apply to private liberal arts colleges, you will likely be asked to write a college application essay (via the Common Application) and smaller writing supplements. These shorter writing supplements differ in length from 250 to 500 words. Questions vary in approach and content, with prompts ranging from "Why do you want to attend Gonzaga?" to "Design your own class for Sarah Lawrence College" or "Choose five words that describe you and explain why." There's a strategy for answering supplemental questions that I teach all of my students. You can find my "Guide to Writing Supplements" at writebig.net/resources.

Finally, if you are applying to highly competitive institutions— Ivy League schools, "Little Ivies," the Claremont Colleges consortium, or other top-tier national universities—then expect to write a lot of supplemental essays. The essay length for these writing supplements may be 100–800 words, depending on the writing prompt. If a school is in your top five, make sure to really take your time creating a strong essay. You can utilize the storytelling instruction in *Write Big* to help you. You can find more resources for how to create memorable writing supplements for top-tier colleges at writebig.net/resources.

Are scholarship essays part of my writing supplements?

In addition to merit aid, most colleges and universities will have additional scholarship opportunities for students. The selection for these scholarships is so varied that you must work with each school to understand them. However, many schools offer scholarship dollars in three ways: 1) in conjunction with your application, 2) as an invitation after you receive acceptance, and 3) accepted by the college but researched and found by the applicant. These scholarships almost always ask you to write an additional essay.

Write Big focuses on how to stand out in your college application essay, but the storytelling techniques and instruction included in these pages are transferrable; in fact, many students included in this book have won additional financial awards applying *Write Big* lessons. If you write more essays for scholarships, whether it's for your college or a private scholarship, I highly recommend you revisit these chapters for guidance. Find tips on writing standout scholarship essays at writebig.net/resources.

Is the University of California's universal application the same as the Common Application?

While many public universities are members of the Common Application, the public colleges of California are not. Instead UC has its own system for its nine campuses and does not require a 500–650-word essay. Instead, you're given *eight* personal insight questions and asked to write a 350-word essay on *four* selections. You can see the current prompts at their website: http://admission.universityofcalifornia.edu.

While *Write Big* provides guidance for the longer college application essay, you will find the storytelling approach essential for answering the UC questions. You can find my guide for navigating the UC prompts at writebig.net/resources.

Should I write an essay if it's labeled "optional"?

My colleague, Dr. Deborah Barany, a fantastic college advisor in Portland, Oregon, tells college-bound students *optional* stands for *opportunity*. Dr. Barany believes every opportunity on your college application should be seized, including additional writing prompts. Often these optional questions ask about an important value the school holds. When you've worked so hard on your application, go this last step as well. While there are no chapters focused on optional essays in *Write Big*, the materials at writebig.net/resources for writing supplements will help you with this portion of your application.

"Once in a while someone amazing comes along and here I am."
—Tigger from A.A. Milne's *Winnie the Pooh*

1

I AM THE PROTAGONIST: BECOMING THE MAIN CHARACTER OF YOUR STORY

When I first met Stephanie, a witty seventeen-year-old with dreams of attending some of the top women's colleges around the country, she was insistent she was the least interesting person on the planet. Stephanie knew this sounded bad and reeked of low self-esteem, but that's not what she meant. Stephanie admitted to being hardworking, having great friends and interesting hobbies, but in her mind she hadn't accomplished anything of great importance, and yet that's the caliber of topic she imagined the college application essay demanded. Without fascinating accomplishments, Stephanie felt her life was unimpressive. "If there was a movie about my life, I wouldn't even qualify as a main character," she laughed. "I'd have to play the sidekick." Stephanie already had me cracking up, and I was convinced her jokes about being boring were impossible. I also knew the key to unlocking her best topic would come from her disarmingly funny and charming personality.

But Stephanie's analogy got me thinking about something else, something I've observed among my writing students for years. Stephanie's belief about her life was like that of many other college-bound seniors—colored by the mindset of writing to impress.

As students imagine writing for teachers, or in this case admissions counselors, ideas take a backseat to pleasing or impressing the audience. But what Stephanie needed, and what many students need, is to step forward to play the role of a lifetime—yourself—and to shed the mindset of the student and embrace the outlook of the storyteller.

The storyteller believes you are already interesting, already ten times more fascinating than you even know, and you are not in competition with anyone else. In fact, the storyteller believes, with the right angle and lighting, there are many, many topics vying for a starring role in your college application essay. If I had to summarize the philosophy of the storyteller it would go like this: there's a hero in every one of us and the story reveals it.

Stepping into the Shoes of the Protagonist

It turns out Stephanie was already the main character, or protagonist, of her life just like you. In fact, you can't *not* be the lead character in your own life story. But the awareness of that role—and the way it can inspire your topic and direction for the college application essay—is what I want to help you discover.

Consider how the experiences from your life—every obstacle, challenge, encounter, failure, triumph, confusion, and epiphany—combine to tell a story of who you are. In literature, the protagonist undergoes what's called moral and psychological growth over the course of the story—this is called character development. So, as we think of your story, and as we search for a topic for your college application essay, we want to zoom in on the moments from your life that formed you. It helps if we think of these experiences as lessons. I'll give you an example from my own life.

When I was a high school senior, I'd already had many significant experiences. I had experienced plenty of positive forces that influenced my identity like competitive gymnastics and honor roll achievements, but also hardships like divorced parents and family with drug and alcohol problems. As I look back and step into the shoes of the main character (me!), I can see important events and positive and negative forces, but if I really zoom in, I notice how certain themes emerge. These themes represent an identity forming alongside the events in my life—sometimes they were connected to events and sometimes they were just my own individuality taking shape. Some of the important ones looked like this: the way moving affected my sense of self, a deep love of language and expression, and femininity as taught by the culture of the American South.

These themes worked somewhat like conversations I had with myself. Moving a lot seemed to create both a confusion and a craving for a sense of home. If I was born in Atlanta, I wondered, but lived in a dozen other places, where was I from? Later in life, I decided to choose my own answer to the question of "Where did you grow up?" Today, I say I am from Jekyll Island, a historic town in the Golden Isles off the coast of Georgia, where our family often took long vacations.

If a longing for home was a nagging question in my childhood, a love of language was more like an answer for my connection to the world. I spent my free time cataloguing the various Southern accents around me, quietly sifting through the pages of the dictionary, or writing poetry in my journal. Language became my homeland.

And while I wasn't exactly sure what town in Georgia, or even in Alabama, I should trace my origin story to, I did know intimately I was from the American South. From the bluegrass music on the radio to the storytelling traditions of my grandparents, even the history lessons taught in school, I learned directly and indirectly about our values. However, my specific training in southern culture was tied closely to being a girl. One of my earliest memories comes from my mother brushing my hair and demanding I stand still. "Beauty must suffer," she said. This saying, repeated by the mothers and grandmothers, female teachers, the old women at church, went on to shape my notions of beauty for many years and seemed to esteem some of the standards I observed all around me—to be pretty was the ultimate prize, even if you must squash your personality, even if it hurts. It's probably no surprise I came to identify later with startling variations of southern female characters like Scout, the fiery, opinionated, verbose narrator of *To Kill a Mockingbird*.

These themes were giving me lessons about myself and about the world. If I listed them all, my life story would create a book of lessons. It's helpful to think of your own life as a book of lessons too. When it comes to the college application essay, thinking this way isn't just a fun activity but a tool for discovering a great topic and writing a unique essay.

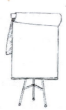

PROTAGONIST PRACTICE

Imagine you are writing a book about your life. For now, just imagine the book is called *I am the Protagonist*. Next, imagine this book will have five to ten key lessons from life—obstacles, challenges, encounters, failures, triumphs, confusions, turning points—that formed who you are today, the very person reading this book. Then, I want you to brainstorm the chapter titles for your book. Titling your chapters is central to discovering your topic because it's the way you narrow down—and emerge as—the main character. In this way, you, much like Stephanie, cannot possibly remain the sidekick.

1. Title your book: *I am the Protagonist.*

2. List five to ten experiences from your life: one from early childhood, two from middle childhood, two recent. *6*

3. From these experiences, create five to ten chapter titles that hint at the lessons. *6 3*

4. Choose three or four titles that resonate with you on some level and write a brief description of the contents and the purpose of a chapter with that title. *3*

Victoria is The Protagonist

In my *I am the Protagonist* edition, here are three example chapters:

CHAPTER 1
I AM ALMOST FROM COSTA RICA

This would be an essay that examines my childhood fascination with telling people I was basically born in Costa Rica because my family moved there when I was three months old. I really, really wanted to be Costa Rican. Why? This essay would explore what it means to be "from" somewhere and how moving a lot as a child shaped the way I see myself today.

CHAPTER 2
RICHARD NIXON IS FROM THE ISLAND OF INCOGNITO

This would be an essay that explores my lifetime obsession with language. Incognito is one of the first big words I remember learning and even though I thought it was a deserted island where Richard Nixon disappeared to after the Watergate Scandal (it actually refers to having a concealed identity), I loved the sound of it. This essay would explore how a love of language has shaped the way I see the world.

CHAPTER 3
LITTLE MISS CINDERELLA MEETS MISS CONGENIALITY

This would be an essay that recounts my bizarre experience in beauty pageants where my victories as most talented and best personality seemed to miss the emotional mark. I would never be Anniston Alabama's Little Miss Cinderella or Cumming Georgia's Miss Junior Miss. This essay would highlight how the disappointment of being perceived as *talented* and *kind* and not *beautiful* or the *best* turned out to be a great message and a pretty good basis for identity. And it just so happens to represent the kind of person I'd rather be today anyway.

As you can see, each of these chapters represents lessons, and I am the main character—I am the protagonist. Certainly, there were other people involved, but the lessons hint that I was the one growing, learning, changing my mind, solidifying my beliefs.

Topic Makeovers

Now sometimes when I ask students to do this exercise, their chapter titles look more like research topics. If that's you, I want to show you how to transform them into lessons to make great topics for your college application essay. Here are some basic chapter titles that need a makeover.

Soccer

Swim Lessons

Getting a Job

AP Microbiology

These topics aren't *bad* topics; it's just they suggest you will write a dry, encyclopedic entry about the subject rather than relate a meaningful experience you've had. It's the experience, *your* experience, that provided the life lessons, values, and a belief system you will take with you to college. What if you approached your topic this way instead?

THE WAY SOCCER LOOKS FROM THE SIDELINES

An essay that examines how an injury gave me a new perspective on the game I love and an opportunity to redefine myself after a lifetime of playing soccer.

HELL DAY

An essay that takes the lessons from the six-hour swim practice my team does once a year called "Hell Day" and translates those lessons from the pool to qualities I use today to solve problems and push myself to a higher standard.

THIN CRUST OR ORIGINAL?

An essay that explores how making pizza is a lot like life—strangely philosophical and full of possibilities.

STREP: A NATURAL BEAUTY

An essay that showcases my love of bacteria and my belief that science gives us opportunities to see the world in a different way. I believe this is an important perspective, and very much needed, in order to solve the problems that exist in the world, something I hope to do in the STEM field.

Spotlight on Vulnerability

If you poll college admissions counselors about what makes a great college application essay, you're likely to hear two words repeated: authenticity and vulnerability. These qualities may seem like a tall order, especially if you don't like writing about yourself. But if you follow the method from this chapter, you will find an authentic topic, a topic only you can write about, and naturally you will become vulnerable. Why? Because the movement from sidekick to action hero in your own life story means becoming brave enough to be yourself.

Stephanie's Solution

In the end, Stephanie found a topic that not only placed her in the spotlight but also showcased her fun personality, as she boldly chose a topic some may consider childish or immature. That's because Stephanie wrote about a Lego city block she constructed in her attic and how she discovered legos as an adolescent, when all of her friends were leaving their play things behind. She writes, "I discovered legos at a late age by most accounts. I wasn't a young child when I began to construct the first portion of Chesterfield. I was twelve. But I consider this a lucky break for me—just when my friends were contemplating careers, getting serious about schoolwork, and growing up, I found something that reawakened the child within me. As my friends lost their creativity, mine grew." As she stepped into the shoes of her own main character, Stephanie drew insights about the importance of maintaining imagination and practicing innovation. Stephanie's investment in authenticity paid off; she went on to receive admission into many of her top choice schools, including Smith College where she now attends. Read all of Stephanie's essay, "The Lego Story," in part III, chapter 15.

For now, here's a look at Nicole's college application essay, "A Whole New World," where she not only manifests as the protagonist but focuses the essay on story itself. You can read all of her essay in part III, chapter 14.

Excerpt from "A Whole New World"

I am going to tell you a little secret. I have assassinated kings, traveled to distant planets, panned for gold, and lived as a pet dog. Of course, having parents die again and again is exhausting; thankfully I have only lived as these characters through inked pages. Books are the adventure that takes no preparation or prior knowledge—just a simple flip of the page. As Mason Cooley once said, "Reading gives us someplace to go when we have to stay where we are." Recently I grew tired of staying put. I was ready to write my own tale, and it couldn't be something as simple as fishing on a lake. My adventure had to be something worth writing about.

My storyline begins early freshman year. The following events occurred: my friend casually issued me an invitation to visit her in Finland; my parents nonchalantly said I could go on the condition I paid my way; I naively checked my savings and found it sorely depleted; I painstakingly proceeded to teach swim lessons for the next two years. Like a tick, I latched on to the idea that I could travel alone, abroad, amongst strangers.

A BACHELORS IN BRAINWORK

Embracing the role of hero in your own life isn't just for your college application essay. In fact, one day when you are off in the bright future leading your very successful life, I hope you look back and see how applying to college was its own turning point or coming-of-age experience. I'd love to someday read the story of how you began to see yourself as the main player, the decision maker, the star in your whole life, even beyond your essay.

College will certainly challenge you with who you want to be, and as you discover, grow, and try on your college self, I want to remind of something: you are already pretty great.

As you look ahead to next year, you might consider how you'll take this current self with you—through meeting roommates, professors, and friends. How your current identity will grow and shift as you read philosophers, work for hours, and perhaps even make and leave romantic attachments. While the work of a college education is most associated with gain'ig knowledge from experts, I'd like you to consider how your undergraduate years will also teach you much about yourself.

How can a growing awareness of yourself help you prepare for college? In the very least, I hope it will help you remember that you're never a sidekick and always the main character of the story you'll write with your life, one experience at a time.

To learn more about what the experts say about a smooth transition into college, visit my resource guide at <u>writebig.net/resources</u>.

THE STORYTELING MINDSET

"Why do you never find anything written about that idiosyncratic thought you advert to, about your fascination with something no one else understands? Because it is up to you. You were made and set here to give voice to this, your own astonishment."
—Annie Dillard

2

(RE) FRESH TOPICS

Samson was a sweet and serious college-bound senior who approached the college application essay already having an understanding of hard work. As a first-team, all-league 6A high school baseball player, he possessed a complex understanding that excellence would spring forth only from a devoted process. Still, he was stuck on one thing: a good topic.

Secretly, I was hoping he'd write about baseball. Samson was a friend of my son, Dezi, and I had watched them play baseball since the days of little league, marveling at Samson's amazing plays from third base. I was eager to show him how to take a topic about baseball and create a dynamite essay. Would he write about the crack of the bat as it hits the ball, in order to address the power and beauty of his days on the diamond? Would he write about the trajectory of a baseball over the outfield wall, as a way of addressing physics, neuroscience, or even metaphorical implications of exceeding expectations?

Okay, maybe I was too into it. Maybe *I* wanted to write about baseball. This happens sometimes as a writing coach—I want to take the topic and write my own essay. Nevertheless, if Samson wanted to write about baseball, I was ready.

However, in the first session of my *Write Big* workshop, Samson gravitated toward an essay topic not about baseball but football, a sport he hadn't played since seventh grade. As his writing coach, I was curious how he could reach so far back for this topic, when the sport he loved and hoped to continue playing in college rested like a glove on his hand. However, as Samson began to explain how the story of *quitting* football, not *playing* football, was something he considered a turning point, I began to lean in.

Many people would have dissuaded Samson from writing about football or baseball, or any other sport for that matter. They might even be saying the same thing to you—you might even hear about it from a college admission counselor. But objectors of what are sometimes considered overdone topics—sports, volunteerism, study abroad, learning disabilities, parental divorce—don't understand two crucial aspects of storytelling:

1. Sometimes the experience really did change your life.
2. The problem isn't the topic but how to talk about it.

I knew Samson had a great topic because he felt quitting football was a turning point in his life. As he explained, he quit something he never believed would come to an end. At the tender age of twelve, Samson was able to see he no longer identified with the rough nature of the sport and the spirit of the coaches. But more importantly to Samson, his essay could address the nature of quitting philosophically and how giving up, a perceived negative, opened a wide door that led to the discovery of new talents, like advanced mathematics and singing in choir, and later, a devotion to the excellence of baseball.

24

How would you like your topic? Fresh or Refreshed?

I like to call a great topic a fresh topic, but Samson's fits under what I call a refreshed topic. Like taking a familiar shirt from your closet and incorporating it into a new outfit, you can take a common topic and show nuanced aspects that are often overlooked. Refreshed topics work like this: take a generic topic (sports) and look at a specific angle (quitting). With this focus, you can impress the reader by creating an essay with a familiar concept and a twist such as, "Quitting: The New Winning."

Fresh topics, on the other hand, are equally ideal for your college application essay. I use the term fresh topic to suggest a subject that's original, authentic, maybe even vulnerable. Fresh can also mean vibrant, alive, or relevant, and it's often the happy byproduct of the "Protagonist Practice" exercise introduced in the last chapter.

If you're wondering how your fresh topic can fit the prompt for your specific college, make sure you've read the FAQs in the introduction section, where I address the different types of college application essays. For now, here are some examples of fresh topics from my students who created an essay for the Common Application.

Grocery Lessons: Three Life Lessons From Grocery Shopping Alone For the First Time

Date with Charlemagne: Historical Subjects Go Viral With Pop Lyrics and YouTube

Math Matters: An Essay About the Way Math Changes How You See the World

Philosophy Talk: An Exploration of Absurdism from an Unlikely TV Philosopher

Live Chicken: How Moving to China at Ten Years Old Transformed a Chicken Into a Brave Young Man

Un Regalo: How an Artifact From a Student's Desk Contains a Hidden Story

Shostakovich 10: A Devotion to Classical Music Training is a Devotion to Learning

Something you'll notice about this list is the way students really considered the admissions audience—and not by way of writing to impress them, but by way of writing to leave an impression. It's hard to forget the essay from a student that begins with him holding a live chicken or a high school student who finds philosophy in animation. In fact, Elijah, the writer of "Philosophy Talk" received a special letter from the Dean of Undergraduate Admissions at Marquette University about the remarkable nature of his topic and his writing.

 TOPIC TRYOUTS

As you move from protagonist practice to topic listing, you want to test your ideas. I like to tell my students to imagine their words and sentences tryout for the essay, but not all of them will make the final cut in the polished paper. If we extend this notion to our college application essay, we can conduct preliminary interviews with our bright ideas to see if they qualify as fresh topics. Use this checklist to decide on one to two promising topics. In part II, we'll use your favorite topic to start writing your paper.

- ✓ Does the topic make me feel bubbly, energized, excited? Could I talk for five minutes without interruption?
- ✓ Is my topic specific? Instead of baseball or learning disability, can I shift into something like Baseball as Philosophy or Three Rules of Any Good Learning Disability?
- ✓ Can my topic be used to show the way I think, how I see the world, or what I care about most?

If you want to read all of Samson's essay on quitting football or Elijah's essay on philosophy, you can find them in part III of this book. In fact, part III may be my favorite section, because I get to show how many students, just like you, found a way to write a unique essay that manages to leave a mark. For now, here's an excerpt from Thea's "Math Matters," an essay on seeing the world through math-colored glasses. You'll find all of Thea's essay in part III, chapter 13.

Excerpt from "Math Matters"

The story begins with a train. It may be an Intercity-Express from Stuttgart, or a Train à Grande Vitesse from Paris, but it's always a train. And on that train, two kids play catch: one of them winds up, prepares to throw, and yet, doesn't move. He, like everything else on the train, is perfectly still. The twist? The train is moving near light-speed, when time itself seems to stop.

That was the kind of bedtime story I grew up with—while other children rode dragons and spaceships, my father and I booked passage on light-speed trains to learn about relativity. The way I see it, I grew up submerged in two languages: German and math. From my father, who wrote his doctorate on representation theory, I gained fluency in mathematics, and from my mother, a clinical pathologist who grew up in Aalen, a small town in Germany, I heard only Deutsch.

A BACHELORS IN BRAINWORK

The capacity to think for yourself isn't just great for choosing your college application essay's topic—it's a great life strategy too. In fact, my belief that thinking for one's self is crucial to learning became the motivation to start my first business with a fellow adjunct professor at the University of Portland in 2013. Cheri Buck-Perry and I began Inscribe after spending nearly a decade sharing an office at the University of Portland. We loved our work teaching writing and literature, but often grew frustrated with students who passively attended classes. There were certainly students who didn't bring their books, even others who didn't bring paper or pen, their desks an entire blank slate. But what really got under our skin were our students who perhaps read the material but seemed neither interested nor curious. Sometimes we were teaching great works of literature, master writers and poets like William Shakespeare, Emily Dickinson, or William Faulkner, yet students behaved as if their minds were as still as a quiet lake, calm and undisturbed. It was like making someone a Thanksgiving dinner and having them say "'no thank you, I'm not hungry.'"

Cheri and I puzzled over this phenomenon often—what we wanted were minds alight with questions, thoughts about passages that moved or haunted them, conversations that explored the recurring themes the authors introduced. In her book, *The Hungry Mind: The Origins of Curiosity in Childhood*, psychologist and director of the program in teaching at Williams College, Susan Engel, teaches "curiosity is an appetite" and argues much of traditional schooling helps students forget they're even hungry. Cheri and I recreated our college courses, rewrote our assignments, and brainstormed how to increase student engagement before we decided ultimately to create programs and classes to reach students earlier in their education. We theorized how cultivating imagination throughout education, not only in the early years of schooling, could actually enhance the analytical skills needed to be better college readers and writers. In short, we sought to foster the kind of student we wanted to someday enroll in our classes. I use to joke with Cheri we should introduce ourselves to parents of younger students as time travelers from the future.

In the end, anyone can do the reading and come to class. Anyone can show up for work. But becoming an independent thinker means to know your own mind and test it against new ideas as you grow. Education at its best does this, but our experiences are often equal teachers. As you move through college and beyond, and consider new theories and subjects alongside your own experiences, occasionally, stop and ask yourself, "Am I listening?"

If you want practice growing your curiosity in a very practical and highly useful way, I recommend spending more time working to expand your vocabulary. How often do we encounter words we don't yet know or words whose meaning we've forgotten? I'm not talking about memorizing multisyllabic words for the SAT but a true expansion of your word bank. Increasing your English language capacity is much like acquiring a foreign language: it's a use or lose endeavor. In other words, if you simply memorize novel words you'll eventually forget them, but if you start to use them, to recognize them in your reading, to notice the relationships between new words and similar words (cue Engel's curiosity research), you can begin the process of keeping these words forever; eventually, they will become yours. The challenge of additional language acquisition may be a reason vocabulary growth is a common goal when I poll college students about their hopes for our course. While confidence is generally the number one goal students want from our writing class, advancing their language base is a surprising second. You can find the five lessons I developed to build a luscious lexicon in the resource guide at writebig.net/resources.

"A spider's web is stronger than it looks. Although it is made of thin, delicate strands, the web is not easily broken."
—E.B. White, *Charlotte's Web*

3

CHARLOTTE'S METHOD: A STANDOUT ESSAY IN 650 WORDS OR LESS

Cooper's application to college demanded the story of his topic. He'd been living with a chronic illness his whole life, which affected his schoolwork long before he'd had a diagnosis or treatment plan. As a hardworking high school student at a challenging, private high school, Cooper had fought for every GPA point. With big plans to attend a competitive, liberal arts college to study business, he needed his essay to offer background to his lackluster grade point average and test scores and to showcase the study skills and work habits he'd acquired along the way. This last part was essential, because it meant proving to colleges he could handle the rigorous and demanding life of a university student.

Ava considered her adoption story central to her identity. Adopted out of Kazakhstan at two years old, along with her older brother, she wanted her essay to tell the story of being raised by a devoted single mother but also to highlight the origin of her learning differences in school. Like Cooper, Ava wanted colleges to understand her GPA represented only one aspect of her identity and she had proven strategies to make her college years a success.

Katherine felt it was impossible to understand herself as separate from her role as the loving, older sister she played in her family. As the big sister to three younger brothers, she designed her essay to compare herself to Wendy, and her brothers to the Lost Boys, from J.M. Barrie's *Peter Pan*, in order to illustrate the way being the oldest shaped her identity. Katherine felt being a second mother to her brothers gave her a window into seeing how all of us are interdependent.

In many ways, these essay topics are what I call origin stories. The word origin means the place where something is derived, and in storytelling, an origin tale seeks to trace our identity backward to a starting point. Although these essays contain origin themes, their topics are quite different. However, when it comes to the college application essay, they share a very important common denominator: telling a life story in 650 words or less. How can Ava or Katherine or Cooper convey the central importance of these stories to their lives in so few words?

Matt had a different problem. As an outgoing and thoughtful college-bound senior from a loving family, he felt he didn't have a central life problem or question to tackle in his college application essay. When he landed on the idea of using his first trip to the grocery store alone as a turning point in his life, I knew he had something fantastic, but I also knew he'd be grappling with translating a feeling, an almost transcendent experience, into a developed essay.

Stephanie, from chapter 1, shared Matt's challenge. She needed to derive meaning from the Lego city block in her attic. Sure, the experience had shaped her, but putting words to feelings that lived only in her mind meant getting philosophical about the value of play. Unlike my students who sought to tell an origin story as their college application essay, Matt and Stephanie needed to birth one.

Birthing an origin story may be too heavy a description for Matt and Stephanie's problems in writing their college application essay and maybe yours too. It's unlikely that Matt's trip to the grocery store or Stephanie's time with legos meant enough to them to give it this weight. But their need to create material, to revisit the evidence of their experience, is likely more accurate. So how did they do it?

These brave and fascinating students are just a handful of examples I could give you, but as a writing coach and a storyteller I see the problem they're facing—too many words or not enough words—as helped by the same solution. Each of these students needed a strategy for telling their story without getting lost in the details of it, while also learning to recognize and maximize the most significant aspects from their experience.

Charlotte's Method

Before I'd met and helped the students from this chapter solve their essay challenges, I'd been working on my own problem. After a decade of working with students on their application essays, my college-bound seniors and aspiring graduate students were receiving regular acceptances into their first-choice schools, even special recognition on their essays. However, I didn't really have a system that guaranteed their results. Instead, I just followed my intuition with each person, helping them create a custom design for their application essays and personal statements. Yet my inner researcher knew there must be certain patterns, traits, and hallmarks each essay shared. So, I began to take a closer look at the most striking examples from my students. Then I began to look at books of published application essays. As I reverse engineered their strengths, I had another epiphany: great college application essays shared some of the features of great literature. The most outstanding college application essays demonstrated the character development of the writer, and I knew I wanted to teach all of my students how to show their personal development inside of their essays.

For the last several years, I've been teaching my college-bound seniors the results from my deep dive on the relationship between story and college application essays. I created a formula I call Charlotte's Method to show how to layer meaning strategically in your essay to demonstrate growth. These layers are the way to highlight the moral and psychological development of the protagonist—you! I named my formula Charlotte's Method because of the way the strategic layering of content ultimately creates the message of your essay. Just how Charlotte the spider, from E.B. White's *Charlotte's Web*, layers silk to create beautiful messages to wow the townsfolk and ultimately save Wilbur the Pig's life, your essay can layer content in such a way to create a message about your life. And this is the trick that Cooper, Katherine, Ava, Matt, and Stephanie all employed to create their standout essays.

Also, it's worth noting when the stress of applications gets too high, remember your goal is to wow admission counselors. Unlike Wilbur who needs Charlotte's webs to save his life, your purpose is to write an essay to give you the most choice about where you attend college, not escape execution. Remembering your college application essay isn't life or death is just one of the ways I recommend staying grounded in this process.

On the next page, you'll see the blueprint of Charlotte's Method. You'll notice I use some original terms here, but don't worry, in part II of this book you'll be learning all about these terms and how to use them to create your own origin story or philosophical encounter or some other mind-blowing experience.

Charlotte's Method Defined

SIDE DOOR ENTRANCE - *Introduction/Paragraph 1*

The SIDE DOOR ENTRANCE consists of a paragraph that focuses on a memory from your life told as a scene or anecdote.

NARRATIVE SITUATION - *Introduction/Paragraph 2*

The NARRATIVE SITUATION paragraph gives background information on both the scene and your historical relationship to the subject.

STORY THREAD A - *Body/Paragraph 3*

This paragraph reveals a specific lesson or insight that stems from your SIDE DOOR ENTRANCE and also relates to another specific aspect of your life.

STORY THREAD B - *Body/Paragraph 4*

This paragraph is another lesson or insight that acknowledges the SIDE DOOR ENTRANCE and goes deeper into another aspect of your life.

ADD IT UP OR STORY THREAD C - *Body/Optional Paragraph 5*

This paragraph allows you to create a list (of sorts) that shows all you've done with the wisdom and insight you've gained since the experience related in the SIDE DOOR ENTRANCE. It's a great place to put all of your bragging because instead of just naming accomplishments, this paragraph can demonstrate how certain lessons from one experience delivered insights you were able to build upon. Or you can just write a third paragraph that creates another STORY THREAD. This paragraph is listed as optional because of the word count issue. Sometimes you don't have space for a third STORY THREAD or an ADD IT UP paragraph.

GRACEFUL EXIT - *Conclusion/Paragraph 6*

The concluding paragraph begins with a reference or "call back" to the opening story to create narrative coherency. The paragraph often hints toward the future and how you'll need the wisdom from the soccer field, grocery store, late nights studying on your bed, and more when you go to college next year. Note: It helps sometimes if you don't tell everything about your memory in the SIDE DOOR ENTRANCE because it allows you to surprise and delight the reader with a little-known fact or missing piece of the puzzle in the GRACEFUL EXIT.

Spotlight: Designer Essays

Once you understand Charlotte's Method you can focus on creating what I call a Designer Essay by using your SIDE DOOR ENTRANCE to harness an original element. Designer simply means that in addition to using this formula you went the extra mile to add an organizing principle to make your essay unique. If you want to see how Designer Essays take Charlotte's Method a step further, see chapter 8, where there are three designs outlined with sample essays. Matt, from earlier in this chapter, wrote a fine Designer Essay you can see there. In Matt's case, he uses the grocery list, or what I call an artifact, to help him develop meaning. In part II, we'll use Charlotte's Method to put your essay together.

Here's an excerpt from Katherine's essay "Wendy and The Lost Boys," where she uses the comparison of Wendy and The Lost Boys from *Peter Pan* as an extended metaphor to introduce the importance of her topic. You can read all of Katherine's essay in part III, chapter 13.

Excerpt from "Wendy and The Lost Boys"

We were sitting in the hall, propped up against our lockers when Caroline studied me and said, "Katherine, if you were a Disney character, you'd be Wendy." My first thought was, really, she's not even a princess? As I quickly ran through the list of Disney beauties before first period, I realized her comparison was startlingly accurate.

As children, Peter Pan's captivating sense of mystery and freedom entices us, but few stop to realize that the key to his whimsical success is his practical partner Wendy. For as long as I can remember, I have been an older sister. I was only eighteen months old when the first of three younger brothers were born. My brothers' names are Jack, Peter, and Matthew, and they have become the Lost Boys to my Wendy. In J.M. Barrie's classic tale, Peter is the one fighting imaginary pirates, while Wendy is the one looking after The Lost Boys. Wendy is the calming presence that holds this band of rambunctious boys together.

A BACHELORS IN BRAINWORK

"But I don't want to be cliché!" Occasionally, I work with students who really struggle with the idea of formula. They see themselves as original, unique, and outside-of-the-box. They would rather go it alone and write an essay that resembles a slam poem than utilize a helpful strategy like Charlotte's Method. And despite my attempts to explain to students the formula itself is just a demystification of story, a tool for approaching a personal essay with a strict word count, and not a rigid structure that defines success or failure, I'm not always successful. Sometimes I pull out my English professor card, but for these thinkers, that's no proof that following the worn path is better than the road less traveled. Interestingly, the last time I had this conversation with a student who rejected both the formula and the examples I shared, in order to go away and write his own masterpiece—who debated the idea there's even a regular pattern to storytelling, who spent weeks stopping and starting and restarting his whole essay—ultimately created a narrative with all the trademarks of Charlotte's Method. Why? Well of course I did not tell him, but he used these ingredients unwittingly because they are the traits of a developed story. They just are. They might be mixed around somewhat and you might say it differently than your peers—I hope you'll do both, actually—but if your essay succeeds, it will be because you've demonstrated growth, much like a character in a novel.

What can we learn from formulas? As an academic, I can tell you that we don't like them much outside of math and sciences. We're okay with theories, but the idea of one truth makes us uncomfortable. And yet, formulas can help us understand the world, even something as specific as the college application essay. For example, in the Charlotte's Method formula we see clearly what was previously hard to see (and for some students it's practically invisible): story + background + specific developments + accomplishments = character growth.

And what of the formulas in our everyday life? Can the support of something like Charlotte's Method mean there are other successful maps and strategies as you continue to develop your own sense of identity and values? Perhaps one of the most useful formulas I've learned comes from the world of habit. Want to stop being late? Look at your habit. Want to improve your sleep? Look at your routine. Want to change your negative thoughts? Consider your thinking patterns.

College is ripe with opportunities for self-reflection, and if you also want self-improvement, I highly recommend learning about habits from the author of *The Power of Habit*, Charles Duhigg. His book demystifies why we do what we do and how to change it if we want. Because no matter how original we want to be in life, we all have some patterns—both good and bad—in common. When we learn how these patterns work, we can undo them for good or use them for good. It all just depends on accepting how the reality of our human frailties, like it or not, makes us our own cliché.

Learn more about Duhigg's research and how improved habits help college students succeed in the *Write Big* resource guide at writebig.net/resources.

THE STORYTELLING MINDSET

"If you don't like something, change it.
If you can't change it, change your attitude."
—Maya Angelou

4

THE "READY, SET" MINDSET

On the first day of classes at the University of Portland, I routinely asked my freshman students to free-write about a series of questions. Before I gave them the list, I'd ask the class just the first one:

What is your relationship to writing?

Our class was an introduction to college writing, yet despite this emphasis students were often surprised by the question. I'd give them a few minutes to take out their paper and pens, before I invited them to begin. Most first days looked like this: two students furiously writing, a few whispering for more instructions from a peer, half of them staring at me in bewilderment, and one student bravely raising her hand for clarification, "You want us to write about *what* exactly?"

If I knew this scene was likely to replay, semester after semester, you might be wondering why I continued to let students struggle. But my approach stemmed from a pedagogical belief—or teaching value—that uncomfortable or awkward discussions often lead to better thinking. It's true, these questions often produced awkwardness itself, but I was okay with that. Because in my classes, I was after something bigger—I was after helping students locate the narrative they told themselves about writing. When students asked, "You want us to write about what?" I felt happy because I knew they were now thinking, even wondering about the meaning of specific words we say every day, like *relationship* and *writing*.

"What's your relationship to writing?" is a tough question because we don't often think of having relationships to things; we generally imagine our relationships are formed with other people. But if you think about it, you'll see you have all sorts of relationships you might not hold in the bowl of your awareness: relationship to money, relationship to food, relationship to body, and so forth. These relationships have influence in our lives whether we acknowledge them or not, but if we wanted to make any long-term improvements in these areas we would first need to assess the health of the relationship.

When it comes to improving your writing or beginning a new writing project, the health of your writing beliefs will not only color the process but shape the final product. So, before we turn the page and dive headfirst into the deep end of your college application essay, I invite you to pause and consider your relationship to writing. Try on the questions that helped my university freshmen find their own answers to their writing narrative.

WRITER'S HEALTH ASSESSMENT

This exercise will take you five to ten minutes, but the awareness will be far reaching because you're likely to expose both confidence and fear, excitement and apprehension, and perhaps you'll even catch what I call a limiting belief. A limiting belief means a story you tell yourself about what's possible. In writing, these limiting beliefs sound like, "I'm just not a good writer" or "I am not very interesting" or "Writing takes me forever." Get all that stuff out, so you can embrace the mindset and the tools that have helped hundreds of students just like you become better writers and start creating their best work.

Write for a few minutes on each question. Narrow in on specific experiences and especially feelings.

1. When you were a kid did you like to read? Tell stories? Draw pictures?

2. When your teachers asked you to write a story in elementary school, did you become excited or did you stare at a blank page?

3. If you wrote essays in middle school or for the first time later in high school, did they come easily to you or was it tough?

4. What have teachers told you about your writing? How do their comments make you feel?

5. Whose writing do you admire?

6. How hard do you work on your writing? What do you think are your greatest writing strengths and weaknesses?

7. As you consider the answers to your questions, which ones do you think will have the greatest impact—positive or negative—on your college application essay?

As you check the health of your relationship to writing, your beliefs about what's possible will affect the results of your common application essay. Let these beliefs wash over you for a minute. They are yours, they exist, and they represent a lot of years and a multitude of experiences. In fact, writing might be one of the oldest relationships in your life.

Now, I want you to pivot and open your mind, maybe even a little wider, to the writing process that's helped hundreds of students let go of their fear of expectations, write better and faster, and ultimately sound smarter. It's based on the simple premise that writing through imperfections—spelling, grammar, sounding ridiculous, uncertainty of thoughts and phrases, can help you write faster. It also means writing in timed intervals with specific benchmarks while simultaneously avoiding corrections. If you want to write a great essay, this approach might sound a little nuts. But we can embrace writing quickly and through imperfections when our goal changes from correctness to creating content. We can also trust we'll create a dynamite piece of writing because it's revision and editing that ultimately make our writing soar (this is the write-better component). Revision and editing steps come later and go a lot faster when we hold them back instead of letting them interrupt the creative process. In the end, the mindset, or new narrative, I am sharing with you can unlock your ideas, jumpstart your writing, beat procrastination, and lead you to some of your best stuff. Are you ready?

THE FIVE RULES OF THE "READY, SET" MINDSET

1 Write Fast. Don't let the finished product intimidate you. Write in ten- to fifteen-minute bursts and then evaluate. Do not evaluate as you go along—it will slow you down. If, along the way, you hear the inner voices questioning *am I doing this right* or *is this even good* or *why would an admission counselor even care about this*, stop. Remind yourself of these rules.

2 Set Specific Goals. Goals should be related to time and objectives. Choose if you want to write for fifteen minutes, thirty minutes, or an hour in your writing session. The answer is your time goal. Then, choose your objective: will I *draft* the first paragraph or will I *revise* the first paragraph? Be clear on your goals, so you don't waste time *writing* and *revising* a paragraph at the same time. Why? Because when you read through it a day later or a week later, you may decide to rewrite half of it or all of it. Now how do you feel about your time, energy, and progress? If you're starting over, probably not great. But if you have goals, then you can move methodically, make real progress, and avoid procrastination. Writing becomes easier and the belief that you'll finish by following the steps becomes reality.

3 **Trust the process.** In the writing process, everything has its place. Don't worry about sounding cliché when you haven't even written an introduction. Don't worry about a conclusion when the body paragraphs don't yet exist. Don't worry about awkward sentences when you haven't completed a paragraph. Clichés can be fixed in revision. Conclusions manifest best when a draft exists already. Awkward sentences are easier to repair when we're not taxing our imagination to both create and reimagine at once. Knowing you'll address awkward phrases, vibrant language, active verbs, and mechanical errors later allows you to write without regret.

4 **Embrace imperfection.** Some of your best ideas are imperfect. But if you change them before they've had a chance to see the light of day, then you won't really ever know them—in fact, you won't have a chance to improve them because, in essence, they won't exist. So, do not focus on perfection in the drafting process. Rather, ignore any thoughts you have about spelling, grammar, punctuation, sounding smart, or even the admission process. These thoughts come later but are unhelpful to getting started and generating content.

5 **Remember Your Training.** The reason I know you can stiff-arm both your limiting beliefs about writing and your fears of the admission process comes from the years of experience I've had helping students create their best writing by remembering these rules. And not just these rules but the lessons I created to go with the "Ready, Set" Mindset.

Composition theorists like Peter Elbow and Donald Murray, along with writers like Joan Didion and Stephen King, have greatly shaped the way I coach writers to first write to discover their best ideas, then return to impose order. However, because your task is bigger than any assignment, with goals greater than the natural satisfaction that emerges from personal writing, *Write Big* is more than the philosophy of how to get started and uncover your best ideas, but a guided tour of how to create a proven, successful college application essay. This book is my way of leading you through the process, and I created it because I believe so much in your potential.

Zane is one such student who needed my guidance to recognize not only the fascinating aspects of his own life but also the step-by-step coaching to create a great essay. Here's an excerpt from his essay, "Ramble On," which draws you into the music of Led Zeppelin and the power of teaching himself how to play guitar. To read all of Zane's essay, go to part III, chapter 15.

Excerpt from "Ramble On"

Led Zeppelin's "Ramble On" opens with a simple, chimy E major chord, wispy like the wind. Although the beginning is relaxing and blissful, the song turns to Led Zeppelin's signature hard rock style by the time the chorus comes. Listening to the song is like an adventure. As I later discovered, Led Zeppelin wrote the song about *The Lord of the Rings* trilogy, one of the greatest adventure stories of the twentieth century. At only thirteen, I sat on my bed and held my guitar in my lap, ready to begin. Surprisingly, the sound was not even remotely similar to the actual song, but I still look back to that moment as the beginning of my own journey and all that I am capable of now.

Since I was thirteen years old, the location where I play guitar has shifted from the edge of my bed to a collapsed, ugly couch, but the act of playing music has become a solitary activity where I can be completely focused and content. Music was once a mysterious thing I felt unable to comprehend. Although I listened to music daily, I had no idea how it worked, much like how most people do not understand how the cars they drive work. I wanted to dissect songs, to examine their unique structures. Having recently moved in with my mom's boyfriend and his three sons, there were very few things that were truly my own. But my guitar and my music were mine, and no one else's.

THREE MINDSET SNAGS TO UNTANGLE

1 If I don't have an outline, I don't know what to write.

Since middle school, most of us have been advised to start with an outline. But in this book, you'll find the outline doesn't come into play until we've started brainstorming and drafting the introduction. This process is related to the genre of essay you're writing. The college application essay is half story and half essay, meaning you must create and analyze in the same writing process. Outlines help us plan, but when we haven't explored our ideas and discovered a focus they're not of much use. Many writing classrooms do not model where good ideas come from, so if you love outlines and struggle with starting without one, try to relax into a process designed to help you discover, plan, write, and perfect.

2 I know my essay needs more but I used all my time and energy constructing the first draft, and now I'm ready to call it quits.

Following the "Ready, Set" Mindset will help you recalibrate your effort, so you work hard in the right places. Novice writers tend to expend the most energy in creating the draft and little time in the creative and revision stages. However, I am going to show you how to write faster by harnessing your creativity in the beginning and how to write better by utilizing the power of revision.

3 I write better under pressure and in one sitting.

The writing process, or the creation of a piece of writing, is not linear, but rather it's recursive, which means it loops back on itself. Beliefs about writing the essay from start to finish without having to go back and make adjustments will leave you frustrated or produce poor quality writing. It's my belief the best remedy to your frustration isn't to write perfectly but to write through your imperfections, knowing they'll be handled at the right time during the process. Imagine if a painter stopped painting to clean up drips or splashes of paint every time she worked on the canvas—how much longer would it take her to finish the painting?

A BACHELORS IN BRAINWORK

Yielding to a writing process isn't just giving over control to your creative side and walking away. It means insisting on both creativity and order in your writing.

The writing process mirrors critical thinking. We acquire new information often in a messy way—without outline or a sense of purpose. But we integrate it both creatively and logically as we ask questions about meaning or imagine implications for new information. In this way, critical thinking is not strictly an analytical process. Despite these skills being emphasized in our classes, critical thinking is also imaginative as we learn to see new pathways.

Not only does the writing process mirror critical thinking, but it also resembles personal growth. As we encounter areas of our lives that seem to demand change, it's unreasonable to imagine thinking our way through it will provide a perfect outcome, much like we can't just sit down and write a perfect essay. And as we try to create change in our lives and experience failures along the way, we must work through these imperfections to grasp the eventual results we want most.

As you think back on your writing experiences, you might notice how imposing perfection on your draft led to a lot of frustration. On the other hand, this sort of straight-jacketed writing experience might have helped you receive a good grade. But I question the cost of your time and energy and perhaps even the strength of your ideas. With so many papers to grade, many high school teachers do not address the quality of your ideas but focus rather on your adherence to instructions. In fact, this may be the reason why you began trying to get it right the first time—because the consequences of leaving out a requirement negatively affected the outcome. However, college classes will be looking for more than checked boxes but at your ideas themselves. How will you be sure the concepts you communicate in your writing are complex and rich enough for this new audience?

The short answer is your ideas should represent your intellectual journey. The longer answer is your intellectual journey comes from the writing process, as you teach yourself what you know or believe along the way. Much like we cannot grow up perfectly without making some mistakes and learning some hard lessons, we can't write a perfect draft straight out of the gate. But the growing-up journey leads to maturity, just like the writing process leads to sophistication. And it's this last part that's the secret to good writing: it isn't that some of us are just naturally better—all of us have messy thoughts and sentences but can improve by using the writer's tools to create a sophisticated piece of writing.

If you want to learn how to harness the power of wild tangents, fuzzy thoughts, or half-baked ideas, use the "Ready, Set" Mindset in all of your writing projects. Learn more about what I call "messy idea theory," and how it can help you become a better writer in the resource guide at writebig.net/resources.

"All the world's a stage, and all the men and women merely players:
they have their exits and their entrances;
and one man in his time plays many parts."
—William Shakespeare, *As You Like It*

5

THE SIDE DOOR ENTRANCE

What does Stephanie's introduction on the town of Chesterfield from "The Lego Story" have in common with Thea's introduction about bedtime stories of trains that travel at light speed from "Math Matters"? What about Katherine's opening story from "Wendy and the Lost Boys," where she explains her discovery that Wendy is, in fact, her favorite Disney princess?

Everyone knows a great introduction is essential for hooking your reader, and if you peruse the college application essays collected in part III you'll notice how they all begin with memorable introductions. But what is the number one quality that makes an introduction stand out? Despite the different topics from Stephanie, Thea, and Katherine, the common denominator is the authors intentionally approach their topics from an angle, and it's the hallmark of the SIDE DOOR ENTRANCE.

Imagine your topic is a house that has multiple entrances. The polite way to enter is of course through the front door, but it's also what's expected or common. In his fantastic book *Writing with Style*, John Trimble explores how academic writing often encourages students to enter through a back door, from a kind of fear of the topic. Because they're not sure how to start, students sometimes make blanket statements about the *world* or *society* or *people*. In other words, rather than speak directly to the reader, they speak in generalities, in attempt to sneak into their arguments. For example, if a student wanted to create an argument to address the narrator's depression in the short story "The Yellow Wallpaper," by Charlotte Perkins Gillman, it's tough to know how to open the essay. The student might try one of these:

"Many people in society believe depression isn't real."

"Depression is a big problem in our society."

"Societal pressures cause depression in most people."

These openers fit Trimble's definition of a backdoor entrance. However, a front door entrance, Trimble's term for an introduction that begins the paper with confidence, great specificity, and style, will engage your reader immediately. In a literary analysis of the narrator's depression in "The Yellow Wallpaper," Trimble would likely remind you there are options for starting your paper. Will you begin by profiling the narrator's symptoms? Outlining gender roles at the turn of the century? Describing the suffocating presence of the wallpaper, an important symbol from the story? If you want to improve your introductions to academic papers, I highly recommend Trimble's book *Writing with Style*, whose chapter on openers may just change your life, not to mention all the other chapters devoted to developing your writing panache.

However, the college application essay demands even more from us than our academic papers. Because we need to write about our lives and submit to a word count restriction, we want to do more than avoid sneaking in through the back door, and instead repurpose our introduction to make an impression. And we can do this by borrowing from the world of storytelling. Storytellers often warm up their audience by telling a little story or describing a dramatic situation while also suggesting the topic.

Entering through a side door means taking the storyteller's approach and applying it to the college application essay. It also means carefully selecting an opening example that represents, symbolizes, or kicks off the conversation the essay will address. A well-chosen SIDE DOOR ENTRANCE provides you with detail to support the analysis that comes later in the essay because it gives you and the admissions reader a common narrative. Think of it: before they started reading your essay you were unknown to them and now you have a shared story, where they are able to see you without having met you. It's that powerful.

Being the protagonist of your narrative is more than an attitude—it means actually placing yourself in the story. Because you can't tell your whole life story in the college application essay, your introduction stands for the moral and psychological growth you've experienced in the last seventeen or eighteen years. In other words, your opener stands in for your life story and the subsequent paragraphs develop the meaning. Easy, right? Okay, I know it sounds like a tall order, but in these next few sections, I'm going to break it down.

It's tempting to see the SIDE DOOR ENTRANCE as *filling* and the rest of the essay as *meat*, but that would mean missing how the opening story can help you write the rest of the essay.

Three Ways In...

There are certainly many ways to write a SIDE DOOR ENTRANCE, but I recommend three story pathways for a strong introduction.

1. Anecdote—A little story that represents your topic

2. Scene—A detailed slice of memory

3. Announcement—Speaking directly to your reader

Anecdotes are like Thea's story that begins "Math Matters." In her little story, she takes us into the world of a narrative, which sounds much like a word problem with an exciting international setting.

> The story begins with a train. It may be an Intercity-Express from Stuttgart, or a Train à Grande Vitesse from Paris, but it's always a train. And on that train, two kids play catch: one of them winds up, prepares to throw, and yet, doesn't move. He, like everything else on the train, is perfectly still. The twist? The train is moving near light-speed, when time itself seems to stop.

Scenes are like the following introduction from Sarah's essay, "Date with Charlemagne," when she describes going through her mom's closet. Sarah's scene sets up her essay about shooting YouTube videos by recasting the lyrics of popular songs into historical facts.

> I was raiding my mom's closet, and I knew exactly what I was looking for. Crawling into the darkness of her wardrobe, I found the floor-length, black gown. I emerged to plunder her jewelry box and extract a pair of dangerously long, rhinestone earrings. To complete the ensemble, I descended to the basement and unlatched my old costume chest. There it was: the princess tiara from Halloweens past. I quickly placed it on my head and raced back to the living room. It was time for my date with Charlemagne.

Announcements are like the next example from Elijah's first paragraph of "Philosophy Talk," when he asks the audience to think about a favorite philosopher. His beginning puts the reader into a philosophical mindset by revealing his favorite philosopher isn't one of the greats but actually a TV writer of some of today's hit shows. His introduction sets the tone for an essay that asks us to question everything.

> Who's your favorite philosopher? Nietzsche? Camus? Kierkegaard? While metaphysics is not exactly a popular topic amongst most teenagers, the circles I run in aren't often characterized as "popular." My answer: Dan Harmon, writer and creator of the hit shows Community and Rick and Morty.

The SIDE DOOR ENTRANCE is elastic, so don't get hung up on which genre. Can an introduction be a scene/anecdote? Yes. Can an introduction be an anecdote/announcement? Sure. Can a good beginning include all three components? Probably. The most important point in showing you the three different styles of introduction is to emphasize how they all work as SIDE DOOR ENTRANCES—they all come at the topic from an angle instead of head on. You'll also notice they hint at some of the essay's themes or tensions, as in Sarah's introduction when she includes fantastic detail and word choice to create a sense of thrill and adventure, just like a scene from *Indiana Jones* yet it's all taking place inside her mother's closet.

Many of the SIDE DOOR ENTRANCES include an element that's like a twist or added layer. This piece is optional, but it does make a great impression on the admissions audience because it shows your awareness that someone, a real person, is reading this essay and you are writing to them. Additionally, if the layer is clever or funny, it shows your personality and also the way you think. If it's optional, why do so many writers use it? Bonus points. Because even while you were painting a picture, placing yourself as the main character in a scene or story, or in Elijah's case establishing yourself as the narrator, you are demonstrating critical thinking. How? Because you're able to show you understand there are other ways to start your essay, but you chose your own way.

Trademarks of a Super Side Door Entrance

- ▶ Approaches topic from an angle
- ▶ Represents or symbolizes the topic
- ▶ Includes rich detail and illustrative language
- ▶ Layers complexity that promotes later analysis
- ▶ Hints at the essay's direction with a clue or question
- ▶ Measures between ninety and one hundred words

KNOCKING ON THE SIDE DOOR ENTRANCE

STEP ONE

Imagine your *topic* is having a conversation with the *experiences* from your life. I know it's a strange request but hang with it for a minute. What would the *topic* and the *experiences* discuss?

For example, what would the topic of *playing with a chronic injury during the last two seasons of varsity baseball* talk about with the experiences of *playing little league, important wins and losses, summer baseball, coach's lessons, support from teammates,* or the *view from the outfield?*

As you sort through your experiences, make a list of possible openers based on the topics you auditioned in part I *and* the introduction pathways listed below. Jot down different moments so you have choices for the steps that follow.

1. Specific moment in time.

Examples: Standing on the stage for the talent show in 5th grade, or a memory from shooting a video pitch to be student body president.

2. Funny fact or story.

Examples: While you hold no official titles or have no scholastic awards, you do hold the record for selling the most tickets to your team's pancake breakfast, or that time you beat your brother in a footrace in the backyard.

3. Memorable word or phrase.

Examples: Your teammates call you "Dezman Dig Dorrito," or your parents nicknamed you "The CEO."

4. Firsts. The first time you tried something.

Examples: The first time you tasted a persimmon, or the time you rode the bus alone for the first time.

STEP TWO

Choose one of the pathways as your tentative opener and try it out as a scene, story, or announcement. Remember the "Ready, Set" Mindset and just go for it, writing for five to seven minutes without worrying about nailing it. In fact, you're testing this as an introduction so don't knock yourself out.

STEP THREE

Evaluate if this introduction has promise as a SIDE DOOR ENTRANCE. If so, what would you change or how would you improve it? Is there a better example from your list? What about your topic? Will this topic work or should you revive your backup topic? Spend five to seven minutes each time you decide to try a new topic or introduction. In less than thirty minutes, you could discover a great start to your college application essay.

STEP FOUR

Use the draft of your SIDE DOOR ENTRANCE to explore your essay's purpose. This next writing is not part of the *essay itself*; instead it's writing *for yourself*, like writing in a journal. Write for another five to seven minutes and answer the following questions. Save this writing for the next chapter on NARRATIVE SITUATION.

- What does this experience illustrate about me?
- As the main character of this story, what qualities does it suggest I possess?
- What aspects of my personality are revealed?
- What does the reader need to know about me (context) in order for them to see the importance of this story in my life?

Finding the right story or scene, not to mention the right words, takes time. Remember you don't have to nail it the first time around because we'll be revising and editing your SIDE DOOR ENTRANCE in later chapters. As you search your memories for options on starting your essay, here's the first two paragraphs from Anika's "Wolfie the Wolf & Me." You'll notice her second paragraph begins with a list, which is the organizational structure she used to convey her theme "life does not always follow our own instructions." You can see all of Anika's essay in part III, chapter 13.

Excerpt from "Wolfie the Wolf & Me"

Wolfie the wolf was the closest thing I had to a human baby as a child. I remember holding her, singing her lullabies, and tucking her in at night. Occasionally, I would stuff her under my shirt, yank her out, and gloriously perform birth. When I was nine my aunt got pregnant, and I was overjoyed. I wanted to hear the whole process. I even went to the baby shower, willingly. What nine year old does that? The answer is a girl who is excited—excited to be pregnant—and have her own children. Becoming a mother has always been my dream, but for now, let me tell you about my current fork in the road.

Plan but don't over plan. Be open.

Today I am a flexible person, but when I was younger I had a plan. When I was thirteen, I had a pain in my side. After many doctor visits, too many blood tests, and one CT scan, I discovered I had MRKH. MRKH, also known as Mayer-

Rokitansky-Kuster-Hauser syndrome, meant that when I was in vitro my uterus didn't fully form. This news meant I would never carry my own children. I felt like a fraud. Instead of fitting in with other girls my age, I felt like there were bright, flashing arrows pointing toward my nonexistent womb.

A BACHELORS IN BRAINWORK

Sir Ken Robinson, an author and speaker on the importance of creativity and learning, explains the concept of divergent thinking as the capacity to see multiple solutions to the same problem. In "Do Schools Kill Creativity?"— which TED Talks list as the most popular talk of all time— Robinson notes that as kindergarteners, 98 percent of us have genius-level ability at this intellectual endeavor, but sadly far fewer students graduate from high school able to hang on to this essential problem-solving approach. The reason children excel in divergent thinking comes from something they actually lack. Young children simply do not think in terms of strict logical explanations for what is possible and so, unlike some adults, turn to imaginative solutions easily. Robinson believes the world needs stronger divergent thinkers to solve the complex problems—poverty, food scarcity, global warming, disease, and many others—we will all face in our lifetime.

The world of college and beyond provides us with multiple disciplines to promote divergent thinking. Literature is just one great example—the ability to see multiple interpretations of the same story promotes Robinson's belief in the power of divergent thinking. Yet even in the literature classroom, students may feel the need to lean toward what the teachers want to hear, not to mention the pressure to squash imagination in the pursuit of deadlines and tests. But what is lost as we do this? In an ever-changing world, a loss of divergent thinking means a loss of understanding, empathy, and perhaps the loss of innovative solutions to solve the problems in our own lives.

In the years ahead, challenge yourself to see stories, new information, and even people from multiple angles and you'll experience the growth of your divergent thinking capabilities. The world sends its gratitude from the future.

Learn more about Robinson's concepts in the resource guide at writebig.net/resources.

"Who in the world am I? Ah, that's the great puzzle."
— Lewis Carroll, *Alice in Wonderland*

6

THE NARRATIVE SITUATION

Jack's college application essay, "Live Chicken," opens with a scene of him inside a wet market in rural China and holding a squawking hen. It's comical, plays off of the special photograph his family keeps of this moment, and the description suggests he'll address something like a culture clash. But Jack's first draft didn't begin this way. He knew he wanted to write about the crazy, chaotic feeling of holding that chicken, but every time he put it into words he went right for the essay's main idea: gaining cultural appreciation. Jack's tendency is commonplace in a first draft, but I knew if he focused on the scene itself, he could create a stronger impression and remove the pressure to make that one moment equal a cultural awakening. In fact, a big meaning like cultural awareness must be developed. The SIDE DOOR ENTRANCE is the first way Jack was able to back off from the obvious, but it only worked because of the second maneuver, which I call the NARRATIVE SITUATION.

As the protagonist of your own story, the NARRATIVE SITUATION is the backstory of the character, and it's what allows you to pack the college application essay with important information about yourself without telling your whole life story.

For Jack, that meant first explaining what he was doing in China. And it turns out the reason Jack's topic is so great is connected to his purpose in living abroad—his family moved there when he was ten. What makes it even more interesting, and continues to paint the picture of the NARRATIVE SITUATION, is Jack's family moved there intentionally, so they could give their family a new experience. Oh, and did I mention that Jack wasn't excited about it? We learn all of this in the second paragraph, not in the first paragraph. Why? Because this strategic layering builds meaning and complexity and causes the reader to reimagine the introduction. Let's call it *The Sixth Sense* effect. If you haven't seen this film, it's a movie that causes your mind to flash through all of the scenes as you integrate the final twist.

Just like the SIDE DOOR ENTRANCE that allows you to wow the admission counselor with the cleverness of a unique introduction, the NARRATIVE SITUATION also adds points to your critical thinking profile because it gives the reader the experience of what, in the writing world, we call development. Development combines two important elements: *showing versus telling* and *complexity*. When Jack explains what his life was like before China, he doesn't just tell us "China was different than home," but rather he shows us the difference with specific examples and illustrative details. This evidence adds complexity because now we re-see the opening scene and understand when the old Chinese women thrust the chicken in his hand and his mom snaps the picture, he wasn't just far away from home but maybe he was missing home altogether.

Let's take a look at Jack's SIDE DOOR ENTRANCE (paragraph 1) and NARRATIVE SITUATION (paragraphs 2 and 3) to see how he does it:

> It's been a long time since I've seen the photograph of me holding a live chicken at the marketplace in Guilin, China. But

even as I imagine it, I feel the blood rushing to my face, as a tiny, wrinkled Chinese woman shoves a flustered hen at me, while I struggle to steady my trembling hands. I see my mom fumble for her phone, and through a clenched smile I plead, "Quick, mom, quick!" Cheese. Click. Flash. The old Chinese ladies howl with laughter, and mom gets the shot.

When I was ten years old, my parents told me we were moving to China. At the time, I didn't even like rice. We didn't move because of a job transfer or in political protest, but because my parents wanted to give us, in my mom's words "a new experience." But who needs new experiences when my best friend lives behind my backyard gate, my soccer team just won state, and the girl I have a crush on likes me back. As a fourth grader, my objections were overruled: I would be starting fifth grade in Shekou International School.

At the Guilin marketplace, we were not only far from Portland, Oregon but far from Shekou. While Shekou is a quick-growing city near Hong Kong, Guilin is a small farming village in the countryside, abundant with picturesque karst hills and rice paddies. The wet-market was the place where Guilin villagers sold their items: fresh vegetables, small fish, bundles of rice, and animals, both dead and alive. If nothing else, my time in China showed me the value of embracing chaos and simplicity because both turned me into a more resilient and capable person.

Remember when I said the formula is flexible? Well, here we have our first example of how that works. As you can see, Jack has two NARRATIVE SITUATION paragraphs. Is that okay? Yes. Does this make his essay better? No. Does it make it worse? No. Jack's strategy does mean his essay must address the other content a little differently later in the essay. He won't have space for an optional ADD IT UP Paragraph, so he gets in a little bragging in his conclusion. All of this works just fine. What I want to highlight in Jack's example, however, is the content he includes. He reveals three important elements in the NARRATIVE SITUATION:

▸ Immediate Context: what (family visit) he was doing at the market (rural village) that day.

▸ Historical Context: his relationship (unhappy) to the topic (moving to China) in general.

▸ Bridge: the last sentence (paragraph 3) that addresses the paper's purpose (dragging me to China not only taught me to embrace chaos and simplicity but it made me resilient and capable too).

So, what's the context of your topic? What background information does the reader need in order to get the significance of your scene?

EXPLAINING YOUR NARRATIVE SITUATION

Take ten to fifteen minutes to draft your NARRATIVE SITUATION. Use the following steps as a guide.

STEP ONE

List the following information to help you write the NARRATIVE SITUATION.

Immediate context

This information relates to your specific situation in the SIDE DOOR ENTRANCE. List out the following, even though you may not use it all: age, year, name of topic, place, feeling, and attitude.

Historical context

This information works as evidence that establishes your relationship to the topic. How did you end up in this particular situation—was it your own choosing or did external influences result in the experience? Was there a build-up of experiences over months or even years that led you to this topic? Think of your topic and ask questions about your long-term relationship to it. Questions might look like:

Have I always been a worrier?

Why hadn't I been to the grocery store alone before?

Why did I start making historical YouTube videos?

How do I justify playing legos as a teenager when I'm supposed to be growing up?

STEP TWO

Now it's time to write your NARRATIVE SITUATION, but we're going to hold off on the last sentence or two, which I call the Bridge. The Bridge works like a thesis statement in the personal narrative essay because it connects the story aspects to the upcoming analysis. But don't write it just yet because you need to plan your essay first. I'll show you how in the next chapter.

Sometimes writers are stumped with how to start writing the NARRATIVE SITUATION, so here are some first lines from the student files. Use them as inspiration for how to start your paragraph. Save your NARRATIVE SITUATION for the next chapter.

Narrative Situation First Lines

When I was younger I was afraid of trying new things for fear of making a mistake.

I first developed an obsession with the creative works of Harmon in the summer prior to my seventh grade year.

That was the kind of bedtime story I grew up with—while other children rode dragons and spaceships, my father and I booked passage on light speed trains to learn about relativity.

When I was ten years old, my parents told me we were moving to China.

Every kid loves getting outside, but for me it represented a way to leave all of my troubles behind.

Some moments in music are extraordinary, like the night I played Shostakovich with the Portland Youth Conservatory Orchestra.

The last example is from Emma's essay "Shostakovich 10." Here's an excerpt from her thrilling SIDE DOOR ENTRANCE and insightful NARRATIVE SITUATION, where you can see how she lays the foundation for the rest of the essay. Can you locate the immediate and historical context in her opening? You can read all of Emma's essay in part III, chapter 15.

Excerpt from "Shostakovich 10"

Every member of the orchestra is fully concentrated and my eyes are glued to Larry Johnson's baton as it cuts through the air. One two, two two, three two, four two. I count in my head the beginning of Shostakovich's tenth symphony, movement number two: Stalin. Sitting up straight at the end of my chair, I inhale. Five two, six two. The bursting sound of four clarinets erupt through the string's unremitting beats with eerie clarity, screaming a depiction of Stalin himself. A furious military snare-drum marches through the frenzy and leads to wails of cellos. As the music intensifies, the collective energy of the orchestra releases my mind from reading notes and an overwhelming feeling of joy and fulfillment replaces my concentration.

Some moments in music are extraordinary, like the night I played Shostakovich with the Portland Youth Conservatory Orchestra. But most of them have been ordinary, like all of the nights I spent practicing clarinet on the edge of my bed. I chose this instrument in fourth grade, simply because my mom's plastic clarinet had been collecting dust in our basement for the last thirty years. So, when in sixth grade, my clarinet teacher suggested that I audition for the Portland Youth Philharmonic, I thought why me? But as a shy twelve-year-old, I nervously auditioned, playing the piece Chrysalis by Gustave Langenus, and to my surprise was accepted into the beginning wind ensemble. I felt like I had been chosen to play in the Hunger Games.

A BACHELORS IN BRAINWORK

Any good psychology course will cover socio-cognitive theory or psychodynamic theory or attachment theory—all psychological theories that help explain how the world and our relationships shape us. In literature, we often examine how a character's environment affects their choices and behavior by looking through the multiple lenses of setting, such as political, emotional, or physical. Growing up in a war-torn society, losing a parent, or living in a city instead of the country, all contribute to how the character develops. And if the story is told in the first person, we may also trace the narrator's beliefs from how they express themselves by studying what's called point of view. In J. D. Salinger's classic novel, *The Catcher in the Rye*, for example, we discover Holden Caulfield's first-person narration shows a juxtaposition between his casual phrasing and the gravity of tragic events in his life. If we want to further understand this mismatch, we might look to Holden's background, or his backstory.

In this way, literary analysis offers us tools for understanding the world around us. Without it, we might think Holden really is lazy when he describes himself this way. But through literary analysis we can discover his character has much more depth and motivation than perhaps even he realizes. Furthermore, by transferring our understanding from stories, we begin to see others differently. Rather than judging someone's actions as simply lazy, we can now imagine other possibilities. We can even imagine there are missing pieces to our understanding of someone's life because in literary fiction authors often withhold information from the story until later in the plot—as we encounter new information about a character it deepens our understanding of their choices and motivations. In this way, the skills of literary analysis are not just tools for reading books but perhaps even tools for understanding people, maybe even ourselves.

In this chapter, we focused on the NARRATIVE SITUATION for your college application essay, but as you finish up the first draft of this important paragraph consider how the NARRATIVE SITUATION provides the reader with a snapshot of the outside forces in your own life, for a context on who you are. I say snapshot because of course there's more to your story. As you move toward your dreams of college, can you align with your backstory? Rather than perhaps wishing, like many of us, to change aspects of our background consider how these forces have equipped you for today, either by offering you tools to develop your identity or shining a spotlight on something you need, something you're still searching for. If there's something missing, what is it? Do you believe you can learn it, get it, have it? As we become aware of these gaps, we learn they are not a death sentence—they are not permanent missing pieces in our lives but rather spaces to be filled with growing, gaining, and learning as we get older.

This last bit of introspection speaks to the power of those inner conversations we have with ourselves on a daily basis. Carol Dweck, psychologist and author of *Mindset: The New Psychology of Success*, has been studying how our internal thoughts shape our ambitions and success. Her book offers astounding stories of all kinds of people both integrating and overcoming their NARRATIVE SITUATIONS to become a healthier, happier, and even smarter person. Dweck even admits when she started her research, she had no idea her own mindset needed a serious adjustment. Through her own work, she learned to change how she thinks and today teaches others how to do the same. You can learn more about Dweck's mindset theories and discover tips to promote a college mindset in the resource guide at writebig.net/resources.

WRITING YOUR COLLEGE APPLICATION ESSAY

"Perfectionism is the voice of the oppressor, the enemy of the people. It will keep you cramped and insane your whole life, and it is the main obstacle between you and a shitty first draft."
— Anne Lamott

7

THE ESSAY SKETCH

We've spent the last two chapters stretching your memory and imagination, so you have material for complex development and analysis. And that also means you're ready to sketch out the rest of your essay. As we leap into planning your paper, breathe and pause. Remember where you are in the process—the development phase—in order to adjust your expectations about the quality of the current writing. Anne Lamott, the author of *Bird by Bird: Some Instructions on Writing and Life*, reminds us that writing takes practice and training, "Try looking at your mind as a wayward puppy that you are trying to paper train. You don't drop-kick a puppy into the neighbor's yard every time it piddles on the floor. You just keep bringing it back to the newspaper." This chapter is all about utilizing the process of writing, the discovery of your ideas, and the training of your thoughts to plan an outstanding essay.

Sketch versus Outline

For personal writing, I like the word sketch because an outline reminds me of high school English papers, requirements, and some degree of forgone conclusion. Instead, if we sketch the final version of the essay, we are freer to make adjustments as we go along.

When I teach students the writing process, I like to show them they can still write even if they don't know everything already. In fact, it's one of the secrets of pushing through procrastination and writing through imperfection. This chapter focuses on showing you how to sketch a plan of your essay by revising your first two paragraphs from your rough draft. This process may seem unorthodox to you but hang with me, and you'll learn how to use your own ideas to help you discover what to say in the body section of your essay.

For our process, the revision of the first two paragraphs is very important before you plan your essay because you want to ensure you've included rich detail, symbolic information, and powerful word choice at the start of your essay; the rest of your analysis hinges on it. Again, you're the creator of the story and the analytical essay writer all-in-one in the college application essay, so let's make sure your opening is ready for analysis.

If you drafted a SIDE DOOR ENTRANCE and a NARRATIVE SITUATION, you're ready for this chapter. If you haven't, turn back now and write those paragraphs because the next set of instructions pertain to the revision of those important paragraphs.

SKETCHING YOUR ESSAY

Part One: Revising Your Side Door Entrance

Read your SIDE DOOR ENTRANCE and ask yourself the following questions. Then, jot down your answers to help you with your revision.

- ▸ What's the main idea of the scene/story/announcement here? How can I make it clearer?
- ▸ Do I include background information that can be reshuffled to the NARRATIVE SITUATION paragraph? Extract this information and set aside.
- ▸ Do I include rich detail or imagery? How can I add words that hint at the main idea? What verbs will bring out the feelings best?
- ▸ How can I use the five senses—sight, smell, taste, sound, and feeling—to create emotion?
- ▸ What can I cut to get the content to roughly one hundred words?

Take a look at the revision of the SIDE DOOR ENTRANCE from Samson's, "Quitting Isn't Always What You Think":

First Draft

The first day of practice was brutal, the sun was beating down and the conditioning was intense. I was going to have to put in more work this season in order to be successful. After four or five grueling hours of practice my friends and I were left sweating and panting. I went home exhausted that night. I woke up the next day to go do it all again. But while my teammates were putting on their helmets, I handed them mine, never to put it on again.

Revision

The first practice of seventh-grade football season began at 10 a.m. in mid-August, two weeks before school started up again. Wearing a heavy helmet made my peripheral vision fuzzy, a familiar but uncomfortable feeling. It was a long day of drills and conditioning in the summer heat and coaches were eagerly watching for the fastest and strongest players. As the smallest on the team, I knew I must work harder for playing time this season. After five demanding hours of practice, my friends and I sprawled beneath the one shaded spot provided by a single tree. The coaches huddled, comparing players on their clipboards. I scrubbed the grass stains off my calves with my fingernails. I shook my one-gallon water cooler, but it was empty. The next morning, I arrived again at 10 a.m. to see my teammates gearing up underneath the shade tree. But this time I walked past them, directly up to the coach, and handed him my helmet. I was quitting football.

In Samson's revision, he focuses on creating the feeling of a hot summer day, sweating outdoors with his team, exhaustion, and very little relief. Notice the series of images in the sentences that precede "I was quitting football." We *see* the "coaches huddle," *feel* the "scrubbed grass stains" taken "off with fingernails," and *taste* the dehydration with the image "shook my one-gallon water cooler." These dismal experiences are intentional and foreshadow the final sentence. Also, notice the "heavy helmet" and "peripheral fuzzy vision." These images become symbols Samson uses to explore how quitting something that didn't fill him up caused him to discover new passions.

Part Two: Revising Your Narrative Situation

Read through your NARRATIVE SITUATION and focus on the following revisions.

1. First line addresses the topic you're focusing on and connects to the SIDE DOOR ENTRANCE.
2. Contains historical context—long-term background information.
3. Contains immediate context—connects to the scene itself.
4. Contains specific details versus generalizations.

Here's Ben's revision of his NARRATIVE SITUATION from his essay on embracing his Asian identity, called "Undercover Identity."

First Draft

This comment was in no way meant to single me out or be mean. The boy who said it was someone who I knew pretty well and actually happened to be Asian himself. The reason this moment stuck with me all this time is because it was the first time I had ever had a reason to feel different from everyone else. In fact it was the first time that I realized I was Asian. Growing up I had lived in the same neighborhoods, played the same sports, and basically lived the same lifestyle as everyone else. I guess somewhere in the back of my mind I always knew, I mean my middle name is Makoto for God's sake, but it wasn't until I reached middle school that the fact that I was Asian really came to light.

Revision

It wasn't really a secret that I was Asian, but it had never really occurred to me before. I knew my mom grew up in Hawaii and that her parents were from Japan. My middle name is Makoto for goodness' sake. It just hadn't been brought to my attention until I reached middle school. Ironically, the kid who high-fived me that day was also technically Asian, but it's not like we talked about it. In elementary school, we measured differences by who was tallest, fastest, or funniest, not racial distinctions. It wasn't that I thought being Asian was bad; I just didn't think any label truly summarized me. For the next few years, I struggled with the contrast of what people said I was and how I actually felt. Looking back, if I were able to give my sixth-grade self some advice, I would tell him not to be so serious and to realize that everyone is different in their own way. I would tell him that learning to accept yourself will allow you to be your own individual who is both unique and likable.

It's tempting to look at both Samson's and Ben's revisions and think, "okay, just make it longer." But the length is just a side effect of adding important content. In Ben's revision, notice the updated first line, "It wasn't really a secret that I was Asian, but it had never really occurred to me before." This line directly addresses the audience's potential confusion about appearance or awareness. Later, he reveals his family's Japanese heritage, but also why he'd gone so long without it being part of his consciousness—and the answer is insightful. According to Ben, when boys are little they are less concerned with ethnicity and more concerned with strength and agility. And you'll notice in the last two sentences, Ben writes the Bridge, "Looking back, if I were able to give my sixth-grade self some advice, I would tell him not to be so serious and to realize that everyone is different in their own way. I would tell him that learning to accept yourself will allow you to be your own individual who is both unique and likable."

Part Three: Sketching the Rest of Your Essay

After your revisions of the first two paragraphs, you're ready to outline the body section and write the bridge sentences. The Bridge sentence(s) works much like a thesis statement and typically goes at the end of the second paragraph or NARRATIVE SITUATION paragraph(s). The purpose of the Bridge is to connect the narrative sections (SIDE DOOR ENTRANCE and NARRATIVE SITUATION) with the body section *and* hint at the essay's overall meaning. Spend five minutes drafting and revising your Bridge sentence (s) because the information gathered here will help you sketch the rest of your essay. Use the following steps to create your full essay sketch.

1 Reread your revised SIDE DOOR ENTRANCE and NARRATIVE SITUATION. Next, free-write for five to seven minutes about some of the main ideas you want your essay to address. Think of these main ideas as lessons, values, or insights. These are *not* the body paragraphs, but your *ideas* for the body paragraphs.

2 Next, look at your first two paragraphs: SIDE DOOR ENTRANCE and NARRATIVE SITUATION. What specific words, examples, phrases, sentences speak to these key lessons? Notice where you have the most connectivity between your main ideas and what you've already written. Write these down.

3 Then, choose your strongest two ideas. These ideas will form your STORY THREAD paragraphs or body paragraphs. You can also use these ideas to help you refine your Bridge sentence (s). For example, one college-bound senior wanted to write about what he learned about love from telling someone other than his family members "I love you." He chose to focus on two lessons: how love brings out the best and worst in people and how love can help someone reach their full potential.

4 Consider how the specific experiences from your first two paragraphs speak to other life experiences. In other words, if love helped this student reach his full potential in his relationship with his girlfriend, how did it influence other relationships? Did he use this personal growth to "love" his friends and family differently? List out your own ideas from your experiences beneath the insights you named in number 3.

5 Now, create a list of accomplishments, turning points, victories, areas of growth in your life that may thematically connect to the main ideas in the essay. For example, if you write a paragraph on how the experience from the SIDE DOOR ENTRANCE helped you gain confidence, what are other places in your life where you've needed to channel the confidence gained from this experience? Title these notes your "ADD IT UP List" and hang on to it, as you'll want these details for either your ADD IT UP

paragraph (chapter 10) or your GRACEFUL EXIT (chapter 11). Of course, they could even form the basis for a body paragraph.

6 Create a placeholder for your conclusion by writing in notes of what might go there. The placeholder is part of the sketch concept, and you might include something like: return to opening story or connect to my dreams for college and beyond.

Below, you'll see an example of an Essay Sketch, where I've filled in the content using Charlotte's Method. Use this example to guide you as your write your own.

CHARLOTTE'S METHOD MEETS THE ESSAY SKETCH

The 1000 Mile Divide: Overcoming Distance and Divorce

SIDE DOOR ENTRANCE
Story of the first time I flew on a plane alone.

NARRATIVE SITUATION
I was only ten years old, and I was flying across the country to see my dad because my parents had recently divorced. I had always been scared of flying, but I really wanted to see my dad.

Bridge Sentence(s): Taking that flight was the first step toward understanding fear and struggle are a part of life and choosing to be courageous comes with surprising lessons and rewards.

STORY THREAD A - *The takeoff is the hardest part.*
Paragraph on how boarding the plane was the height of my anxiety but I soon learned that everyone there wanted to help me. I learned you're only as alone as you think you are. This experience was fresh in my mind as I did

a student exchange last year. Not only was I traveling without parents, but I was not fluent in the language. Because of my belief in the support of other people, my experience was life changing.

STORY THREAD B - *Turbulence is a real thing.*

The stormy relationship between my parents added a lot of fear to the flight. From this I learned things I'm often afraid of simply represent other fears and rarely can be isolated to something as simple as flying alone. My parents' stormy relationship has improved just like my fear of flying, but from it I learned to race to conflict, rather than waiting for resolution to come to me. This belief really helped me when our basketball team was having internal strife. As the team captain, I led our team through tough talks but also fun outings to create the unity we needed. Finishing second place in state was only one victory that year.

ADD IT UP

Since that flight, I've faced other fears: tried out for a play, learned to drive a car, and given a speech to my high school. I've also found a love of helping others resolve conflict and work as a peer counselor at my school.

GRACEFUL EXIT

Great ending goes here…will likely talk about how college will be a new challenge filled with some fear of leaving home and maybe even turbulence too. Roommate joke? Thoughts of studying abroad.

From Sketching to Drafting

An essay sketch means you've harnessed your best ideas to imagine content for each paragraph, and it also means you can start writing the whole thing! But if you want to go a step further to create a standout impression, make sure to spend time in the next chapter, which shows you how to use design principles to write a more sophisticated essay. For now, here's an excerpt from Sarah's essay "The 24-Hour Riddle," where she uses the SIDE DOOR ENTRANCE and NARRATIVE SITUATION to set up the framework for solving the problem of too little time in a day. Notice how her intentional number references signal the brain to think mathematically and how her active verbs "assign," "prescribe," and "add," further contribute to her word-problem themed introduction. Her NARRATIVE SITUATION and subsequent paragraphs use timestamps to thematically address her essay's topic. Read all of Sarah's essay in part III, chapter 15.

Excerpt from "The 24-Hour Riddle"

Sarah attends school for 7 hours a day. Her teachers assign 2 hours of homework nightly for each of her 4 courses. Sarah's doctor prescribes 8 hours of sleep in order for her to be healthy. But dance rehearsal adds 1 hour to each school day, not including drive time. There are only 24 hours in each day, but student government, community service, and youth group can add at least 1 more hour to any given day. Sarah must still include: 1.5 hours for eating, at least 1 hour with family and friends, and 30 minutes for personal hygiene. Never mind if Sarah's grandparents stop by. What should Sarah subtract? How will she decide?

6:09 AM: the exact minute my alarm has been sounding for the past six years. During this time, I have been following the prescription for being a good kid, reaching higher than the standards expected of a teenage girl, and chasing after personal passions while balancing my life as a student. At some point, however, I began to question the writers of this math problem. In calculus, we call this type of dilemma "the solution does not exist." Yet, most successful people are constantly juggling family, work, and school, while solving world hunger on the side. American culture glorifies busy.

A BACHELORS IN BRAINWORK

What keeps many of us from starting an important writing project? The great mystery of how to go from blank page to great piece of writing likely tops the list. Surely, many of us have learned about prewriting, outlining, and drafting but somehow these don't seem to solve the problems we encounter when we write. How many times have you had a great idea but when you sat down to write, your epiphany dissolved into disjointed prose?

We all wish writing was linear, yet its recursive nature confounds us. But only if we let it. Rather than avoiding writing because we fear the black hole of our time and commitment, we can actually harness the messy aspects of writing by breaking it into steps or stages, just as this chapter introduces.

Recently, a much younger friend of mine said, "I'm trying everything, but I just can't seem to get ahead. Why can't there just be a map that shows me the way to my future career and mate? Where's the map to happiness?"

Writing is a lot like life. While there isn't a map of life that leads directly to a destination, it is possible to relax and recognize that you are the map, or in the very least, you are writing the map with your life. And while we can't know the final outcome or ensure there will not be losses and setbacks along the way, we can predict a positive outcome with a commitment to finding our way with the help of our principles, guidelines, and trusted advisors.

The process from this chapter is much like this philosophy. We can only go so far before we stop, evaluate, reflect, and plan the rest of the essay. Like sketching a draft, applying to college is but one stopping place along the map. For example, it would seem that once you gain acceptance into your ideal college and start your higher education you'll just take one step at a time, until you've arrived. But talk to most college seniors, and they'll explain how now they're making even bigger decisions and facing a lot of uncertainty. It's possible such a report fills you with fear, but I encourage you instead to accept this might just be how life works. And if that's true, it'll mean defining happiness in such a way that you can find fulfillment even amidst uncertainty, challenge, and fatigue.

How do researchers define happiness and what can college students learn from them? Learn more in the resource guide on this very subject at writebig.net/resources.

WRITING YOUR COLLEGE APPLICATION ESSAY

"Make it simple but significant." –Don Draper from *Mad Men*

8

DESIGNER ESSAYS

How did Matt make an essay on grocery shopping complex and original? How did Sarah make an essay on her love of history personal? And how did Stephanie make an essay on the Lego city block in her attic sophisticated?

First, Matt, Sarah, and Stephanie reached these heights in their college application essays by being intentional. They each wanted to create an essay that stood out among other applicants, and they knew it would require a strategy to make that mark.

Next, they created college application essays to harness the power of the content to inspire the structure of the essay. If you've heard the adage great writing is the relationship between form (organization) and content (main ideas), that's what this chapter is all about. If this section feels too advanced or overwhelming and begins to weaken your writing process, don't worry: you don't have to do any of it now, or maybe at all. Just read the chapter and let the material go to work in your subconscious. In other words, don't feel you have to create a Designer Essay *now* because if you're still up for it *later*, these embellishments can be added in revision.

A note about process: Creating a Designer Essay means embracing the messy aspects of the process. You may read the sample essays in this chapter and have a eureka moment and plan your whole essay around your epiphany. Or you may simply follow the steps to plan your essay and have a breakthrough later in the writing that helps you give your college application essay its designer attributes. Either way is fine. The point of this chapter is to expose you to the important relationship between form and content and how to intentionally harness that power to create a dynamite piece of writing.

Designer Templates

The following essays introduce three methods for designing your own: metaphor, artifact, and theme. It's not so important which method you choose—in fact, there are certainly other categories. But for now, take a look at how these writers formed a Designer Essay around one of these concepts and perhaps think about how to model your essay around the inspiration these student essays provide. At the end of this chapter, you'll find an exercise to help add design principles to your essay. Adding style, originality, and complex critical insights makes you a multi-dimensional storyteller. Admission counselors will take notice.

Method 1: Design Based on a Metaphor

Sarah's essay uses the extended metaphor of PR—or public relations—to introduce the author's love of learning and explore the lessons she takes from it. In public relations, agents seek to make celebrity clients look good by remarking on more of their good deeds than the bad press they often receive. Additionally, they may sometimes spin a celebrity's poor choice into a narrative or try to deflect attention. See the notes in the outline for how Sarah extends this metaphor effectively.

Through page 101: On the left page, you'll see the student examples labeled using Charlotte's Method. The right page includes corresponding notes to the elements of Charlotte's Method, along with further explanation of how each writer creates a successful paragraph.

DATE WITH CHARLEMAGNE

I was raiding my mom's closet, and I knew exactly what I was looking for. Crawling into the darkness of her wardrobe, I found the floor-length, black gown. I emerged to plunder her jewelry box and extract a pair of dangerously long, rhinestone earrings. To complete the ensemble, I descended to the basement and unlatched my old costume chest. There it was: the princess tiara from Halloweens past. I quickly placed it on my head and raced back to the living room. It was time for my date with Charlemagne. SIDE DOOR ENTRANCE >

When I first met Charlemagne, I knew he needed my help. I was thirteen, and he was 1,269, but it wasn't his age that was the problem. What I couldn't understand was why his legendary exploits failed to inspire the same fascination in my middle school peers as they did in me. The guy discarded more wives and mistresses than a Hollywood leading man and had more kids than the Duggar family on TLC. He could have dominated today's tabloids, yet the dust of time covered Charlemagne like a shroud. NARRATIVE SITUATION 1 >

Side Door Entrance

Behind-the-scene narrative of making a historical music video with a twist: her date's name is Charlemagne—the first Holy Roman Emperor.

Notice the adventurous or historically-themed verbs that help set the stage for her passion for history, which will be unpacked by the author later— raid, emerge, plunder, descend, unlatch, race. These verbs are no accident.

Narrative Situation 1

"Any modern PR maven would consider Charlemagne a lost-cause client, but I took him on with relish."

Later in the essay, Sarah will directly address the PR metaphor as seen in the quote above. But in this paragraph, she hints at it, when she speaks of reviving Charlemagne by playing on his bad boy side, while also hinting at Charlemagne's identity for the uninitiated. The hint is important because it presents the problem that a public relations agent can solve: this guy needs a makeover.

"The dust of time covered Charlemagne like a shroud" is a fantastic image that illustrates the problem and maintains historically-themed language.

Before middle school, reading books had satisfied my fascination with history. But learning about the first Holy Roman Emperor inspired me to bring history to life. Any modern PR maven would consider Charlemagne a lost-cause client, but I took him on with relish. Maybe my friends weren't interested in him on paper, but what if I brought him to life through something to which all teenagers could relate, popular music? NARRATIVE SITUATION 2 >

And so, I decided to fix history's public image problem. I transformed the lyrics of popular songs into lessons that resurrected historical figures and eras. With the help of Garage Band, I recorded myself singing the new versions. I donned costumes like my mother's black dress and used a camcorder to direct myself as onscreen talent. A bit of editing with iMovie, and my finished music videos were uploaded to YouTube. "Charlemagne," a rendition of Lady Gaga's "Telephone," was soon followed by "Incalicious" set to "Fergalicious;" "California Gold" set to "California Gurls;" and "Galileo" set to "'Dynamite" by Taio Cruz. Sometimes I searched for the right songs. Sometimes they found me. When a serendipitous alignment between modern rhythms and encyclopedic facts occurred, things just clicked. STORY THREAD A >

My friends and teachers loved it. People around the world loved it. I was surprised by how much I loved it. Sharing my work and passion felt great. There was nothing better than hearing classmates singing my lyrics as they walked through the halls at school or reading the messages that poured into my inbox from thousands of followers as far-flung as Japan, Germany, and Brazil. Teachers throughout the country incorporated my videos into their history curriculums, and even TED Talks referenced my endeavors. STORY THREAD B >

Narrative Situation 2

This paper has two background paragraphs that establish the topic's relevance. The second one is the historical relationship plus the Bridge.

Historical Relationship: "I've always loved history, but middle school showed me that I wanted others to love it too."

Bridge: Overtly introduces PR metaphor and reveals that her videos were the solution to solving this problem: "Any modern PR maven would consider Charlemagne a lost-cause client, but I took him on with relish. Maybe my friends weren't interested in him on paper, but what if I brought him to life through something to which all teenagers could relate, popular music?"

Story Thread A

"I decided to fix history's public image problem" with PR techniques. In this paragraph, Sarah introduces evidence on "how" she began to solve history's public image problem. By listing names of songs and artists, along with types of video and editing equipment we not only see how she set about accomplishing her goal, but also that she is an innovative problem solver.

Story Thread B

"Turns out I love PR because I love learning and sharing. And guess what? Others loved it too." This paragraph deepens the analysis because it shows a surprising satisfaction with the results. In other words, she accomplished her goal, but the way it impacted more than her peers was an even greater reward.

This paragraph also allows her to do some bragging that's relevant to the topic. Additionally, it foreshadows how she'll use the knowledge discovered here to solve even bigger problems in the world.

As educators repurposed my videos, I began to discover my own purpose. Sure, I was good at making videos, but I uncovered other passions too. In starting a chapter of the United Nations Foundations Girl Up campaign at my high school, I became a PR agent for a segment of society even more disregarded than the subject of history: adolescent girls in low-income countries. I was named a Teen Advisor and International CoChair of the organization, and even spoke at the United Nations about my advocacy for teenage girls—girls who are as ambitious as Charlemagne, as brave as Joan of Arc, and as clever as Cleopatra. Girls who deserve to make their own history. ADD IT UP >

My YouTube videos are now a thing of my past, as I have shifted my focus from the intrigues of the past to the challenges of the present. But I still reflect on these creations and sometimes jot down new lyrics. Occasionally, I even try on that black dress. And just the other day, I turned on the radio and thought how much Ke$ha's "Tik Tok" sounded like "Plymouth Rock." GRACEFUL EXIT >

Add It Up

This whole PR experiment helped her discover there are other, maybe bigger, problems she'd like to help bring into the spotlight, like working as a global PR agent for girls' education around the country. This tie allows her to bring in her very impressive experience of starting a United Nations chapter of *Girl Up* as well as speaking before representatives of the UN. I especially love the way she ties together her experience representing nameless young girls around the world with famous names from history we know and remember. This paragraph showcases higher-order thinking because Sarah is able to highlight sophisticated relationships among otherwise very distinct categories.

This paragraph also helps her include (and brag more) about some of her biggest investments and accomplishments. It's worth noting in the first version of this essay she actually just wrote about paragraph 6, without the storytelling frame created in the essay you're reading today.

Graceful Exit

Narrative reconnects to opening—YouTube videos—to hint at future aspirations, while still showing it may be impossible to turn off her "inner PR maven," with the Ke$ha reference.

Method 2: Design Based on an Artifact

Matt's essay, "Grocery Lessons" uses what I call an artifact—an item from the past—to create a structure. The body of the essay is organized around the items on his grocery list, subtly introduced in the SIDE DOOR ENTRANCE and used as the Bridge in the background paragraph. He pairs lessons with the items on his list. See the outline notes to learn how he uses his artifact effectively.

GROCERY LESSONS

As I turned the wheel, I felt the lip of the curb hit my tires as I parked in the farthest empty spot from the grocery store. I walked through the half-empty spaces, rechecked my pockets, and studied my phone: "Fruits, coffee creamer, chicken." I stood at the entrance. And as a woman exited through the automatic doors, the cold air conditioning awakened me to another error: I'd forgotten a cart. I turned around. A few seconds later, I finally walked inside—this time feeling prepared and a little more comfortable, since I had something to hold onto. SIDE DOOR ENTRANCE >

On a warm Saturday this September, I sat outside on my patio steps hoping to find anything to occupy my time. My mom walked outside to get the daily mail. She noticed something was wrong, and I simply responded that I was bored. As a stereotypical Italian mother, she began aiming meaningless ideas at me, while I kept brushing them off. Then the worst of all came. She suggested I go to the grocery store and quickly rattled off a list. Strangely, at seventeen years old, I had never been to the grocery store by myself. As the youngest of four children, going to the grocery store had only ever meant tagging along and staying close to the cart. Now as my role changed from a cute cart passenger to paying customer, the fear truly struck me. I looked at my list one more time and began. NARRATIVE SITUATION >

Side Door Entrance

Behind-the-scene narrative—just before he enters the grocery store, Matt uses his scene to emphasize his nervousness. The artifact is first introduced when he says: studied my phone.

Notice the words that convey uncertainty—farthest empty spot, half-empty, rechecked, studied, stood, error, forgotten, turned around, finally walked inside, something to hold onto. This feeling of uncertainty is important to the development of the main idea in the essay.

Narrative Situation

Explains why he's at the grocery store and his nervousness: he's never been there alone. He points out the unlikelihood of this situation with emphasis on his birth order—the youngest.

Bridge: "Cute cart passenger to paying customer" hints at the essay's literal and figurative direction. He cements his artifact when he says "looked down at my list." This inclusion is very important because it prepares us for the innovative design with titles.

Apples: My first stop was the produce aisle. I was determined to look like an expert. I tossed a few Fujis into the air trying to remember my mother's instructions. A good apple is heavy or light? I chose the lighter one and ripped off a plastic bag, dropping it smoothly inside. I later learned that I should have picked the heavy apples. In the end, however, it didn't matter which apple I chose, rather it was that I was making choices. Participating, it turns out, is more fun than watching. STORY THREAD A >

Coffee Creamer: My next stop was more complicated than my last. Not only is the dairy aisle in the back of the store but the aisles are the narrowest. I glanced at the list but noticed she did not specify which coffee creamer. Coffee-Mate or International Delight? Carton or plastic bottle? Hazelnut or Original? After blocking the passageway for five minutes, I realized many unhappy people were waiting. I hurriedly grabbed original. As I rolled my cart away, I noticed that the pressure to be polite caused me to make a quick decision. Luckily, it was only creamer. But as I thought about politeness, I realized it is not always the correct answer, especially when the stakes are higher. STORY THREAD B >

Story Thread A

Item 1 on the list: Apples. The author tells the story, and then offers analysis.

Notice the pattern of story and then analysis that he uses for the three STORY THREAD paragraphs. It begins here.

Story: "I was determined to look like an expert. I tossed a few Fujis into the air trying to remember my mother's instructions. A good apple is heavy or light? I chose the lighter one and ripped off a plastic bag, dropping it smoothly inside."

Analysis: "I later learned that I should have picked the heavy apples. In the end, however, it didn't matter which apple I chose, rather it was that I was making choices. Participating, it turns out, is more fun than watching."

The last line of the analysis is a callback to his Bridge: "cute cart passenger to paying customer."

Story Thread B

Item 2 on list: Creamer. Tells story, then offers analysis.

Story: "Not only is the dairy aisle in the back of the store but the aisles are the narrowest. I glanced at the list but noticed she did not specify which coffee creamer. Coffee-Mate or International Delight? Carton or plastic bottle? Hazelnut or Original? After blocking the passageway for five minutes, I realized many unhappy people were waiting. I hurriedly grabbed original."

Analysis: "I hurriedly grabbed original. As I rolled my cart away, I noticed that the pressure to be polite caused me to make a quick decision. Luckily, it was only creamer. But as I thought about politeness, I realized it is not always the correct answer, especially when the stakes are higher."

Chicken: My final stop was the deli counter. Before I left the house, I received a short lecture to order thinly-sliced chicken, not turkey. My mother proceeded to tell me that the butcher would warn me that thinly sliced chicken falls apart. I shrugged it off then, yet when I politely asked the butcher for mom's precise requirements, he warned me that it does indeed fall apart. I ordered it anyway. I laughed when I realized my mom, once again, was right. But I also recognized the value in insisting on what I want. Unlike the dairy aisle, I hung with the discomfort as I advocated for myself. STORY THREAD C >

I clicked the button, the garage door opened, and I parked the car. My mom waited with anticipation, but I confidently unloaded the groceries. After all, I had already led my senior class's twelve-mile pilgrimage, powered through three brutal football seasons of daily doubles, and survived two weeks in Nicaragua. Nonetheless, the trip to the store felt like a small but significant personal achievement. I feel ready for whatever comes next. Still, I hope she doesn't ask me to get the Thanksgiving turkey. GRACEFUL EXIT >

Story Thread C

Story: "Before I left the house, I received a short lecture to order thinly-sliced chicken, not turkey. My mother proceeded to tell me that the butcher would warn me that thinly sliced chicken falls apart."

Analysis: "I shrugged it off then, yet when I politely asked the butcher for mom's precise requirements, he warned me that it does indeed fall apart. I ordered it anyway. I laughed when I realized my mom, once again, was right. But I also recognized the value in insisting on what I want. Unlike the dairy aisle, I hung with the discomfort as I advocated for myself."

This last line connects his final lesson with his first one, demonstrating personal growth even with the trip to the grocery store.

Graceful Exit

Matt transitions to a conclusion by going back to parking his car, this time in the garage. Also, his confidence has returned. He ends by joking about Thanksgiving—as in, "I nailed this one, but I am still a novice." His joke contains humility, which demonstrates critical thinking because it shows awareness of the audience. In other words, he's gained a lot of confidence from the grocery trip, but he wants to show the admission counselor that he understands this one trip to the store is an example, not his actual transition into manhood. However, another stroke of brilliance in this essay is the way it shows how ordinary experiences have meaning and contribute to our maturity.

This final paragraph also includes ADD IT UP details such as football practice and leading his senior pilgrimage. These mentions are intentional to demonstrate the grocery store experience is a simple story, but he also knows a lot about dedication (football) and leadership (senior pilgrimage).

Method 3: Design Based on Theme

Stephanie's essay, "The Lego Story," from chapter 1 uses the theme of innovation to introduce her discovery and fascination of Lego cities but also to illustrate the way she sees the world. Themes are subtle messages woven in our writing that emerge for readers—unlike metaphor, often they are unspoken, as you'll notice in her essay she only mentions the word *innovation* once. See the outline notes to learn how Stephanie incorporates theme within her essay.

THE LEGO STORY

The man is about to propose. It's going to be perfect.

He's figured it all out: the music, the lighting, the shiny golden ring, even the restaurant, Palais de l'Amour. He must make her say yes, because he has everything planned perfectly. Suddenly, he has a sharp vision of their wedding day—she'll wear the dress sold in Clasco's Emporium down the street, beside Barney's Pet Shoppe. They will marry in Chesterfield's Town Hall, built in 1891, and the photographer will take pictures that will never be developed. But that's okay—that's what happens when you're a lego.
SIDE DOOR ENTRANCE >

I know what you're thinking: legos are simple blocks you played with as a child. Maybe you built a dysfunctional car or a staircase into the air; these are strange topics for a seventeen-year-old girl's college application. But this perspective shows only a partial view of legos. Nothing reveals this more than the intricate Lego Creator™ city block in my attic. Each citizen of this two-foot-long town has a complex backstory—a family, a house, a personality. But the best part? With legos, you are given creative license to change these things.
NARRATIVE SITUATION 1 >

Side Door Entrance

Scene/Anecdote Blend: A story about a man who wants to create the perfect proposal with a twist: he's a lego figure. This twist is our first introduction into our innovative narrator. Stephanie's storytelling ability draws us in with images like "shiny golden ring" and names of places like Chesterfield, Clasco's Emporium, and Barney's Pet Shop. Later when we learn the town is an invention, we further appreciate Stephanie's imagination, as she's not only built a town with legos but created a universe.

Narrative Situation 1

This paragraph blends announcement with backstory. It addresses the reader's questions about legos as a serious topic and embeds background information about the Lego city block in her attic. Stephanie begins by immediately addressing the surprising topic, "I know what you're thinking: legos are simple blocks you played with as a child." Then, she introduces the theme of innovation when she speaks directly to readers (announcement) about their expectations regarding legos, "But this perspective shows only a partial view of legos." In other words, she's saying, "When I see legos, I see more than tiny, plastic blocks." Additionally, the lines, "But the best part? With legos, you are given creative license to change these things" illustrate Stephanie's belief: the creator's role is to think imaginatively. She is also foreshadowing an innovative maneuver coming later in the essay, when she reimagines the opening lego character right before our eyes.

I discovered legos at a late age by most accounts. I wasn't a young child when I began to construct the first portion of Chesterfield. I was twelve. But I consider this a lucky break for me—just when my friends were contemplating careers, getting serious about schoolwork, and growing up, I found something that reawakened the child within me. As my friends lost their creativity, mine grew. NARRATIVE SITUATION 2 >

Every new book of instructions presented challenges that could not be solved by asking the teacher or copying off the internet. When the rule book was wrong, I had to improvise. When the design was faulty, I decided to change it. Sometimes I utilized my experience to reconstruct a defective window, door, or even an entire floor plan. Sometimes I added flourishes to buildings of my own accord or furniture where there was none. While in class, I learned to color inside the lines (or, rather, build inside the lines); at home, I was free to construct or change whatever my mind desired. STORY THREAD A >

Take the man in the restaurant, about to propose. Strip away his shiny ring. Bring him outside the building, on his knees, arms outstretched. Now he is a beggar, holding out a plastic cup in hopes someone will donate to the cause. Or, move him up several stories, above the restaurant, into the apartment. Here he creates masterpieces of artwork, which are sold all over town. One even hangs in the mayor's office. Through what some would call play, I learned innovation, creativity, and just a little bit of rule breaking—because when I changed the job or position of the characters, I went against the rulebook that demanded they stay put. STORY THREAD B >

Narrative Situation 2

This paragraph gives us specific information about her time spent building with legos and establishes another layer of relevancy: she discovered them later in life. This admission adds an additional level of innovative thinking—she is not limited by artificial boundaries like age or what her friends think. She writes, "But I consider this a lucky break for me—just when my friends were contemplating careers, getting serious about schoolwork, and growing up, I found something that reawakened the child within me. As my friends lost their creativity, mine grew." Stephanie doesn't believe "getting serious" and "growing up" should replace creativity or play, something commonly believed by teens.

Story Thread A

Stephanie directly addresses innovation by explaining how she had to consistently use her own imagination to create. She juxtaposes a book of instructions against her own brain. In other words, she's not only intelligent but she's aware creativity is an important life skill.

Story Thread B

This paragraph is an innovation on a main idea—our writer just can't do things by a script, even a good one like Charlotte's Method. But that's okay! I love how she makes it her own and keeps with her theme. In other words, STORY THREAD B is like a second scene or a SIDE DOOR ENTRANCE part 2.

Here, she provides a live illustration of innovation by taking you back to the opener and changing the story. She doesn't tell you how to imagine this—she shows you.

There are other rulebooks in life that have challenged me to innovate in ways I never imagined. For two summers, I taught kids of all ages how to swim, according to a 200-plus page manual. "What do I do with it?" I remember asking. "You read it," my manager told me. "And then you memorize it." She then informed me a new manual would be issued every year. I learned very quickly that the rulebook was incomplete, failing to cover challenging scenarios. When a child in my class was an adept swimmer, but a poor listener, the book demanded I pass him. I realized that following the manual was not only wrong, but could actually put a child in danger. STORY THREAD C/ADD IT UP >

As I gained confidence in my teaching style and myself, I realized that no matter how many manuals life hands me, they cannot tell me everything. Sometimes, life requires you to build outside the box. What started with legos blossomed into a different way to look at the world—through a window tinted with creativity. GRACEFUL EXIT >

Story Thread C/Add It Up

This paragraph includes a specific experience that connects to the bigger picture in her essay: how teaching swim lessons was a kind of innovation. Rather than list out a series of accomplishments, Stephanie, like Sarah from "Date with Charlemagne," zooms in on a particular experience to show us a relationship between creative thinking and play and something more sophisticated like thinking for one's self.

Her STORY THREAD/ADD IT UP hybrid demonstrates the writer's awareness, which further deepens her critical analysis. It's like she's saying, "Sure innovation helps you with legos, but you can't just play all the time." Much like Matt from "Grocery Lessons" who includes football practices and leadership experience, Stephanie wants to assure readers she has a serious side too.

Finally, her example (teaching swim lessons) shows she can transfer information from one thing to another—this demonstration illustrates very high-order thinking—it's essentially a whole paragraph of synthesis, or the blending of two different examples in order to show a connection. See chapter 9 to learn more about synthesis.

Graceful Exit

Stephanie uses the word "manual" to get us back to the lego theme (legos come with a book of instructions). She also asserts innovation is an essential life skill and builds confidence and a lively world view. The line "Sometimes, life requires you to build outside the box" is one of Stephanie's final innovations, as she blends two sayings, "think outside the box" and "color outside the lines" and adds a lego twist with the word "build." The final sentence returns to the image of the window as an homage to the lego city buildings in Chesterfield.

DISCOVERING THE DESIGN IN YOUR IDEAS

Using design means to intentionally create a pattern in your essay. As you consider how you might add one of these designs to your own essay ask yourself if your topic can be organized based on any of the following principles. As you discover ways to add meaning to your essay by incorporating a pattern, fill in your Essay Sketch from chapter 7 with your new designer ideas.

- Broken into parts or categories, e.g. components of an engine
- Viewed in layers or as a kind of recipe, e.g. pie crust
- Planted with an essential item, e.g. a grocery list or a catcher's mitt
- Ordered based on numbers, lessons, colors, observations, rules, e.g. the Three Rules of Camping
- Considered based on genre, e.g. musical notes or theories
- Compared to something else, e.g. finishing a race or a working as a PR agent
- Tied together with a theme, e.g. courage, grit, imagination

A BACHELORS IN BRAINWORK

Many of us have the mistaken belief that good writers are born naturally talented. Some of us may even think a love of science or math makes some people strong in those subjects but lacking in others. I believe this myth stems from the way certain individuals can naturally or intuitively *see* what's happening behind the scenes with writing or language while for others it's just more mysterious. But mysterious doesn't mean we can't learn how to write better, sometimes much, much better, nor does it mean we can't learn to see patterns in writing. What does seem to be true is that everyone who wants to become a student of good writing improves.

As you move through your college career, remember the wisdom of this chapter on writing a Designer Essay. Focusing on the relationship between form and meaning comes after focusing on a plan. Why? Because focusing on the plan provides an immediate feeling of success. When it comes to writing it's important to feed the machine lots of good feelings—your mental outlook and the time spent writing are permanently intertwined. You can't separate them, even if you wanted to.

Once you have a plan and tons of good feelings loaded into the machine, then it's time to ignite the creative centers of your brain and imagine the precise shape of the writing project. Spending some time in this area is meant to be fun, to remind you how writers create masterful prose. If it feels stressful or like you're straining, move on. Writing is an organic process meaning as you write you will make new discoveries.

Designer Essays teach you how to plan a college application essay, but what about an argumentative essay or a research paper? Can you use design principles for these traditional assignments? Or for other instances of personal writing? To learn how to use design in all of your writing, read more about what John Trimble, the author of *Writing with Style* introduced in chapter 5, calls clean narrative line. Most students understand clean narrative line to be the topic sentences and transitions in their writing but knowing the function of these writing elements is not the same as utilizing their purpose. Instead, strengthening the narrative line means creating strong relationships between paragraphs. I've been teaching high school and college writers how to augment their narrative line in everything from research papers to personal essays, and the results have been overwhelmingly positive. In fact, I believe a writing project can sometimes improve by a whole letter grade when the writer learns how to harness the power of the narrative line. Learn the secrets of a strong narrative line and how to utilize them to improve your college writing assignments in the resource guide at writebig.net/resources underline.

WRITING YOUR COLLEGE APPLICATION ESSAY

"I was born good but had grown progressively worse every year."
—Scout from Harper Lee's *To Kill a Mockingbird*

9

STORY THREADS

When I first met Thea, she was already a highly accomplished student, nominated for a National Merit Scholarship and vying for admission into some of the top colleges in the nation. In the middle of application season, as she was comparing the astrophysics programs at Wellesley College, Columbia University, Rice University, and Macalester College, she also flew to Germany for a conference and completed her application for National Merit semi-finalist. On paper, she was one of the top students in the country, and in person she was an absolute delight. Thea loved to talk about books, movies, friends, her German mom, her mathematician father, her study-abroad experience, and so much more. I wondered about what tied all of these subjects together for this remarkable young woman; what was the common denominator? Within fifteen minutes of meeting her, I would learn. The winning topic that kept emerging was something most people would never consider for a college application essay because it's just too basic, especially for an Ivy League application. But it was undeniable: Thea would write about math.

Math had shaped the way Thea saw the world, built her confidence, and fostered her desire to study astrophysics. She had the math stories (and the math jokes) to prove it. But what about the rest of the essay? How could she build meaning in an essay that focused on a subject both simple and entirely complex?

I introduced you to STORY THREADS in chapters 3 and 7, and you've had a chance to see student examples in "Designer Essays." This chapter is devoted to helping you craft original STORY THREADS you'll weave throughout the body of your essay. STORY THREADS bring clarity and specificity to your essay and are the reason this writing project is called college application *essay*, not college application *story*.

If you've learned to write an analytical essay in school, or an essay on a novel, you'll be most familiar with this section of the paper. However, because it's personal you might not immediately see the connections. The STORY THREAD script that follows the next section is an excellent guide to help write your body paragraphs.

Story Thread X-Ray

Let's look at a STORY THREAD paragraph from Thea's "Math Matters" to demystify how a STORY THREAD paragraph creates a strong analytical paragraph that maintains a narrative sound.

> As a rule, the first time you face some mathematical concept, there's a high probability that you won't understand it. [1]In order to understand said concept, you have to keep at it, and doing so means putting up with this incomprehension. [2]And so from math I learned resilience. I learned to live with discomfort, and more importantly, I learned the necessity of this tolerance. [3]This doesn't just apply to math. Knowing that I can tolerate discomfort gives me the confidence to push myself and explore outside of my comfort zone, like when I

spent a semester at a boarding school in Germany. [4]Ultimately, I know that I have the resilience to survive it.

[1]**Topic Sentence:** The STORY THREAD in a succinct sentence.

[2]**Context + Example:** A little background information or a blend of context and example. "Incomprehension" is the example she highlights from the broader topic of "math."

[3]**One or two sentences to develop meaning about the STORY THREAD.** This part often adds or highlights something in your STORY THREAD. Thea highlights how incomprehension creates discomfort and shows how discomfort leads to tolerance.

[4]**Two or three sentences of analysis or synthesis.** Thea offers analysis when she connects the way confidence leads to discomfort, but she deepens her analysis when she does what I call *synthesis*. Synthesis is the connection or blending of experiences or examples. She not only says she's gained confidence from math (which she's gained from the discomfort born from resilience—can you hear all of those layers?) but also that it is connected to her willingness to spend a semester five-thousand miles away from home in a German boarding school; synthesis shows Thea is able to make deep connections with her topic. In this way, synthesis is the height of analysis because it shows you can see complex relationships with simple subjects. And with only 650 words or less, it's a great way to stand out!

Story Thread Script

- ✓ Relevant to the topic
- ✓ Begin with a topic sentence that hints at the paragraph's direction
- ✓ Provide context prior to example
- ✓ Highlight a specific example
- ✓ Spotlight a characteristic from example for development
- ✓ Synthesize analysis to make connections

SCRIPT YOUR STORY THREADS

1. Read two more STORY THREAD excerpts from different writers.

2. Use the STORY THREAD Script as a checklist to identify the elements from the STORY THREAD Script in each example.

From Zane's essay, "Ramble On," on learning to play guitar.

> Music demands thinking outside the box or, as psychologists call it, divergent thinking. Recognizing multiple solutions to the same problem develops over time. I may have been able to speak the language of this foreign land, but with a heavy accent. Songs sounded stiff, forced, and artificial. Oftentimes, the most obvious way to play a song was not the best way to play it. I soon realized that one had to adapt to the style of each song. It had to sound natural, and it was the small, obscure touches that perfected the sound. Not surprisingly, divergent thinking is also applicable to real-world problems outside of music. In computer science, one is presented with a problem and is tasked with finding the most efficient way to solve that problem. Both the musician and the computer scientist must be capable of recognizing the less obvious of these solutions and putting them into practice.

From Brian's essay, "Turf Lessons," on the merits of a hard work ethic on the soccer field.

> The first thing I learned from squaring up against players three years older and seventy pounds heavier is this: if you think you're going to get crushed, you're going to get crushed. A

lifetime of competitive soccer brought speed, skills, and a sense of the game that veteran players couldn't anticipate. It's hard to get crushed when you're sprinting around them. I've seen my experience with soccer translate directly into schoolwork. When my google calendar illuminates tomorrow's date with a test in first and second periods, a presentation in fifth, and a soccer game later, the uphill battle feels impossible. I remind myself what's possible and go one step at a time. With this inner motivation, I've learned to believe in myself. I still follow my dad's motto, with an added implication: capability comes from hard work, but self-belief is the hidden strength behind it.

3. Write 2-3 STORY THREAD paragraphs by using this script to jumpstart the process. These blanks work like a parking attendant pointing you toward the empty spaces. If you find better parking along the way, follow your instinct. But ultimately return to the STORY THREAD Script to verify you've added all of the elements, which add up to illustrate your critical thinking.

Topic Sentence _____

_____

State Main Idea in Succinct Sentence

Context + Example _____

_____

_____

Background information + specific example to evidence main idea

Analysis _____

_____

_____

_____

Example + Main Idea + How it Works

Synthesis _____

_____

_____

_____

How it works—to make connections to a) your bigger topic b) a related topic

Note: It's not necessary to make outside connections in every STORY THREAD.

Don't worry if your STORY THREADS are a little frayed around the edges. We will be addressing revision and editing in chapter 12. In the meantime, I hope you'll continue to take inspiration from the student writers. Here's a STORY THREAD excerpt from Cade's "Family Ties" essay, which examines the growing pains of becoming a blended family.

Excerpt from "Family Ties"

My cooperation and flexibility were not polished over a sixteen-hour drive but more like a couple of years. In my new family setting, rather than a "yours and mine" policy that had worked with just my brother and me, I had to be open to change. One of the first things to go was my individual toothpaste, which soon became shared amongst multiple siblings. I had to adjust to the harsh mistreatment of my toothpaste, the squashed tube now smothered in germs. I learned to let it go. Around this same time, I transferred into a new school district, which also meant a new basketball team. The recent relationships skills I gained came in handy as I developed good chemistry with my team in only a short time.

A BACHELORS IN BRAINWORK

Occasionally, I find myself in one of those intellectual conversations about the merit of a college education. Devil's advocates press that a college education isn't necessary to compete in today's world, and with the rising cost of education, it might actually be economically disadvantageous to graduates. I admit the cost of higher education is something to be greatly considered by any young person looking to take out student loans or fund their university education, but whether or not one goes to college altogether often comes back to a central notion I just can't shake. For me, the overall value of moving through your education with peers, many of whom will share your interests and age, is this: the power of a college education comes down to teaching you how to see, locate, connect, and evaluate complex information.

Surely, you are doing some of this before college, so what is it about a college education that's different? Well, for starters you'll now be engaging in this sort of thinking independent of the requirements of school. You do not have to go to college, so just this change of context is significant. Furthermore, this ability to think for one's self—to choose—by sorting through the deluge of choices, options, and opportunities that come your way throughout life is an intangible reward of a thoughtful college education.

Why did I include the word thoughtful, just now? Because completing a college education doesn't mean submitting to an intellectually transformative process, much like finishing a paper cannot guarantee you've learned the material. Taking the time to engage with challenging readings, asking questions when content exceeds your immediate comprehension, comparing classroom knowledge to the outside world, and being surprised, even corrected, by new information ultimately combine to create intellectual transformation. It's true, you will always find highly-degreed individuals, sometimes even your bosses or leaders, who seemed to have skipped the personal transformation I believe a college experience provides. I suppose it's just another reminder that college itself cannot give you this; personal growth while in college is something you sign up for and see through.

But don't just take my word for it. If you want an eloquent, powerful, and viral description on the power of a college education, please read what *Time* magazine calls the "best commencement speech of all time" from author David Foster Wallace. In "This is Water," Wallace narrates the wonder and strength *possible* from a college education and the intangible benefits that exceed a college diploma.

I used to assign "This is Water" to my university students on our final day of classes. Few were graduating but it was my way of saying, what you learned here about how to think, how to read, how to write, it's not just for writing papers. It's for life. It's forever. If you're fortunate enough to attend and graduate college, take it with you. You can find Wallace's speech included in the *Write Big* resource guide at writebig.net/resources.

WRITING YOUR COLLEGE APPLICATION ESSAY

"I don't know how to put this but I'm kind of a big deal."
— Ron Burgundy from *Anchorman*

10

ADD IT UP

When Davis applied to college in 2015, he was eighteen years old, just like most college-bound seniors. However, if you looked at his remarkable life experiences, he seemed much older. For example, at eighteen years old, Davis had already flown a plane, climbed a mountain, and built a drone. With so many accomplishments, you'd imagine Davis grew up as a daring and confident child. But if you read his college application essay, "Ticket to Ride," you'll discover these heights came only after he got over his fear of trying new things. Here's how Davis begins his essay.

> I fidgeted with the quarters in my pocket, ensuring I had each and every coin to make it across the city. The bus stopped, and I jammed the slippery, jittery coins down the slot and gave the driver a look I hoped said "I have done this a million times." With the bus's pneumatic hiss, my little bit of confidence left rushed out. I had never ridden the bus alone before, but the time had come to attempt it. I was eleven years old, my parents were at work, and I had to traverse Portland and cross

the Willamette River to get to the dentist's office. The bus driver handed me a ticket, and I scuttled and stumbled as the bus jumped onto the road.

There are many notable qualities in Davis's SIDE DOOR ENTRANCE. For starters, you'll notice there's intentional word choice around the feeling of nervousness, with words like "fidgeted," "slippery, jittery coins," and "scuttled and stumbled," while words and phrases like "make it across" and "traverse" suggest the concept of journey. Next, not only does Davis stress about the journey ahead, he worries he'll be outed as a first-timer. And finally, Davis foreshadows that while the experience wasn't perfect, it was successful.

You can read all of Davis's essay in part III, and in it you'll learn from his NARRATIVE SITUATION and STORY THREAD paragraphs his fear of new things has a backstory, yet this scene marks the first time he experienced the feeling of triumph associated with risk, and it serves as a turning point in his confidence.

What follows Davis's STORY THREAD paragraphs is an intentional stacking of accomplishments in a paragraph I call ADD IT UP. This paragraph has many forms, but ultimately allows you to accomplish one or more of the following traits in your essay:

1) Add up the meaning of your essay to showcase stronger analysis (also known as meta-analysis)

2) Include a big accomplishment that if unleashed earlier could appear as overt bragging

3) Combine accomplishments and analysis to evidence growth.

I named this rhetorical maneuver "ADD IT UP" because it strikes me that it's a bit like showing your math: show how the development of your character produced real results. In Davis's case, it looks like this: trying new things + feelings of confidence = making bigger choices and greater rewards in his life.

Here's Davis's ADD IT UP paragraph.

> I hardly ever think about that day on the bus, probably because I don't take it anymore. I now drive a car. I wasn't thinking about it on the day I woke up at 1 a.m. to attempt to climb Mt. Hood with my dad or when we built a quadcopter together for a physics presentation. I wasn't exactly thinking about it on the day I flew a plane, but I sure experienced some of the same feelings, the fright of trying something new and the rush of confidence that came with success. However, I might be thinking about it next fall when I first walk onto a college campus, needing to find my classes and remembering how to make friends.

In Davis's ADD IT UP paragraph, he's able to impress his readers with these surprising accomplishments, and the way he ties the achievements to "that day on the bus" shows the admission counselor *he* sees the connection. This tiny phrase speaks loudly because Davis's awareness evidences real growth—in other words, he can look back on his own life and be insightful, which means Davis is smart and mature. In his last sentence, when he writes, "I might be thinking about it next fall," he hits the mark for meta-analysis, where he sees his simple experience of riding the bus has relationship to not just past accomplishments but future experiences when he'll once again feel like that nervous kid. The line also shows humility, as Davis admits that although he's done great things already, starting college will challenge him once again. Davis's humility makes him likable, and we just can't keep ourselves from cheering for this adventurous college bound senior. Allow me to add it up for you: in this one paragraph admissions counselors meet an accomplished young man who's driven, insightful, smart, mature, humble, and also likable. And his strategic placement of this paragraph is part of the charm—he doesn't open with climbing a mountain or flying a plane but with feeling scared on a bus.

Do You Know Who I Am?

The ADD IT UP paragraph is one of the secrets of writing a comprehensive essay in 650 words or less. Like the NARRATIVE SITUATION which condenses our backstory, this paragraph also saves us from telling our life story and removes the pressure to ensure readers know of our vast and impressive awards right away. The ADD IT UP paragraph solves this problem by giving you an opportunity to carefully choose and concisely express your talents and achievements, in order to give the admission counselor insight into who you are as a whole person, not just as a student. This lean paragraph also deepens your analysis by strategically placing achievements after you've already evidenced main ideas and demonstrated vulnerability.

Sometimes you're able to integrate your accomplishments into body paragraphs, or you just don't have room and therefore need to blend your "braggable outcomes" into the conclusion. Please know it's not required to dedicate a whole paragraph to the ADD IT UP component, but if you don't include it, make sure you know why. In other words, make sure your reader gets a clear understanding of the kind of person, student, sibling, or co-worker you are in the other paragraphs by integrating some of these remarkable details from your life.

YOUR BIG DEALS + YOU = AWESOME

Back in chapter 7 during step 3 "Sketching the Rest of Your Essay," I asked you to create a list of accomplishments and milestones and to title it ADD IT UP list. Return to this step and sift through your list. Follow these steps to write your own ADD IT UP paragraph.

1. From your list, which accomplishments spotlight a strength related to your essay's overall topic? How could you incorporate them in an ADD IT UP paragraph?
2. Read the following examples and note how the writers incorporate their accomplishments.

From Elijah's Essay "Philosophy Talk":

> Their world is far removed from mine, but the lesson still translates. Rick and Morty fostered a jumping off point for my own ontological introspection, and I began to rethink what I want out of life. Since seventh grade, a lot's changed. I'm no longer that lonely kid, cooped up in his basement. I've moved to my room. My younger self sought material wealth. Profit supplanted my happiness. After considering absurdism, I realized there's no reason for me to pursue money and a seventy-hour work week if it'll make me unhappy. This paradigm shift has driven me to pursue an intellectually rich life. It's why I debate. It gives me an opportunity to explore profound ideas in an intellectual community. It's why I write music. It provides a creative outlet that pushes me beyond my self-perceived limitations. It's why I pursue economics and political science. I seek to better comprehend what drives the world around me. Each lens is an insight into the enigma of life and that search is fulfilling.

Here, Elijah connects his analysis of Ricky and Morty, the topic that encouraged philosophical inquiry, with other ways he's challenged himself. Elijah shows how this kind of introspection eventually led him to a sorting process, to evaluate what he loves most—debate, music, economics, and political science—while considering what he's outgrown. Elijah illustrates how this reflection revealed a change: he no longer wants to pursue a career promising wealth if it costs happiness.

Elijah's ADD IT UP paragraph adds significant value to his essay because of the esoteric nature of his topic (TV shows and philosophers) and his SIDE DOOR ENTRANCE. While comical, his opening portrays him sitting on the couch watching TV episodes and thinking about philosophy. Since his end goal is to achieve admission into his top choice school, it was important Elijah add in the academic details to show he's a well-rounded student.

From Samson's essay, "Quitting Isn't Always What You Think"

> Giving up football didn't mean I gave up athletics all together; instead I had more time to dedicate to baseball. The abilities required to be a good baseball player turned out to be in my skill set, much more so than football. Baseball is a sport where it doesn't matter where you come from and what your physical attributes are, but rather how hard you work and how focused you are. A common saying, and something that I truly believe, is that baseball is 80% mental. I played on the diamond in the spring, summer, and fall all the way through middle and high school. More important than the scores and the plays are my teammates. Together we battled Portland spring weather spending countless hours pouring dirt, raking, and weeding Clopton field so that we could play some ball. Transcending the long weekend trips and late night comebacks, my baseball community encouraged me to focus to be the best I can, not just as an athlete but as an individual.

Like Stephanie's "The Lego Story" and Sarah's "Date with Charlemagne," from chapter 8, Samson chooses to focus on one example to make a larger "ADD IT UP" point. Because his essay examines how quitting football changed the trajectory of his middle school aspirations, you might think his shift was exclusive, from athletics to academics. However, in this paragraph not only does Samson reveal he continued with sports, he illustrates how the football work ethic translated to his life as a baseball player. Moreover, he shows the admission counselor he knows a lot about grit—something not always associated with quitting or giving up—as he highlights practices and the long days spent working the baseball field. In this way, the ADD IT UP paragraph allows you to develop complex meaning by taking a strategic layer introduced earlier (quitting football) and demonstrating how this choice fostered growth and maturity (quitting one thing doesn't mean he can't keep commitments or is afraid of working hard).

3.   There are so many ways to ADD IT UP. Write your own using these examples as inspiration. Note the structure of the ADD IT UP paragraph is similar to the STORY THREAD paragraphs, except the ratio of example is higher than analysis. Also, remember you may end up folding your ADD IT UP paragraph into a STORY THREAD or the final paragraph, the GRACEFUL EXIT. Because of the strict word count of the college application essay, absorbing the ADD IT UP paragraph may be necessary.

As you leave this chapter, which focuses on gaining insight from your achievements, I want to give you another excerpt to remind us of the importance of vulnerability. The ADD IT UP paragraph allows for overt bragging because we've already opened up on a personal level. Here's an excerpt from Gillian's essay "Born on September 11th" whose SIDE DOOR ENTRANCE does just that, as she foreshadows how her essay will grapple with making sense of an unwanted life experience. You can read the entirety of her essay in part III, chapter 13.

Excerpt from "Born on September 11th"

My fifth birthday was important. This is not chiefly because it was my *birthday*, nor because my mother had made my kindergarten class homemade cupcakes the night before. No, the significance of that specific birthday is due to the fact that I was born on September 11th, 1996. Five years later to the day, perspectives, world-views, and lives changed for millions of Americans. Meanwhile, a five-year-old girl sat at a dining room table in Portland, Oregon and blew out candles on a cake.

A BACHELORS IN BRAINWORK

The phrase "ADD IT UP" likely reminds you of simple math, where you put together numbers to equal a sum. At this point, you've also likely discovered that unlike math, which generally has just one answer, the world of literature provides you with multiple outcomes. I've heard many readers lament the difference between straightforward mathematics and the so-called hidden meanings in stories and poetry.

However, if we change the phrase "ADD IT UP" to "show your math," your mind may begin to see how the world of math and literature are not opposites. There are many ways to reach the same answer, just as there are many interpretations of the same lines from a poem. Additionally, we may experience the same events as someone else in life, even someone our same age, and have a different outcome. Why? Well, to extend the math metaphor, there are variables. These conditions shape us all differently, despite our wish to believe in maxims like: hard work + determination = success. If you've ever worked hard for something and failed to win, you may know what I'm talking about.

When I ask my college students about their greatest lessons and surprises in the college experience, they often tell me positively they didn't know how different their peers would be from them—they didn't know how differently the world can shape individuals or what it would be like to have great advantages or disappointing setbacks like the new people they've met in college. As you encounter difference—whatever it looks like—in the years ahead, I encourage you to remember how in stories math won't always give you the same sum. Is there a way to predict the differences and how they lead to specific outcomes? Many psychologists are studying this very question today, including Angela Duckworth, author of *Grit: The Power of Passion and Perseverance*. Duckworth's research shows the qualities of outstanding achievement have more to do with persisting through challenges and less to do with overall talent. She even reveals how some rigorous colleges use a kind of "grit test" to score applicants for admission.

To read more about the psychology of personality and success and take Duckworth's *grit test*, check out my article on this topic at writebig.net/resources.

WRITING YOUR COLLEGE APPLICATION ESSAY

"But Max stepped into his private boat and waved good-bye
and sailed back over a year
and in and out of weeks
and through a day
and into the night of his very own room
where he found his supper waiting for him
and it was still hot."
—Maurice Sendak, *Where the Wild Things Are*

11

THE GRACEFUL EXIT

All the hard work of the college application essay, but it's still not done. If it were an analytical essay for your high school English class, you'd probably know what to do. Many are familiar with the formula: repeat thesis statement, highlight your sub-arguments, and leave us with something to think about. But in personal narrative writing, especially for the admissions audience, how do you wrap it all up?

The GRACEFUL EXIT is my name for the conclusion of your college application essay. After all, you made the SIDE DOOR ENTRANCE in order to stand out, so now you want to leave us with equal panache. But unlike the SIDE DOOR ENTRANCE, where the point is to tell a story and make us see and feel your experience, the GRACEFUL EXIT relies on your ability to tie up the loose ends as you remember your purpose: to attend college next year.

From Davis to Anika to Samson to Thea, you're not the first student to look at the empty space of the conclusion and wonder what goes there. I didn't include this script in chapter 7 when you designed your essay because you still had so much to write and uncover. By now, I hope you haven't just made some important connections in your essay but some important connections in your life.

PREPARING FOR YOUR GRACEFUL EXIT

Follow this outline to create a GRACEFUL EXIT to tie up all the loose ends and establish how your essay fits within the context of your life.

- First line reestablishes the narrative and connects to the introduction
- Two to four sentences of "highlights reel" of big ideas from the essay
- Final line alludes to how you'll use these skills in college next year or ends on a light note with a joke or wink from something you've already said in the essay

As you can see from the GRACEFUL EXIT outline, these pieces are malleable. Besides the first line referring back to the narrative, you have a lot of flexibility with how you move the pieces around. Like this chapter, conclusions are often short. You only have 650 words, so it's not uncommon to have a ninety-words-or-less final paragraph. Here are some examples of GRACEFUL EXITS. Remember, all of the sample essays included in the chapters can be found in their entirety in part III.

From Davis's Essay "Ticket to Ride":

> That fateful afternoon in the summer of 2008, I hopped off the bus and walked down the block towards the dentist's office breathing a sigh of relief. My parents asked me later that day how it went, and I played it cool, not making a big deal out of my bus adventure. I got over my fear of new experiences on that day and began calling them adventures instead of ordeals. It began the process of molding me into an independent young man who pursues life with a passion for learning new things and with the ability to put the reward of risking failure over the possible embarrassment that comes with first times.

From Jack's Essay "Live Chicken":

> Much has changed since that first day in the Guilin marketplace. My family no longer lives in China, or in Dubai (which is where we lived post-Shekou), or treks the globe to places like France, the Philippines, or Oman. In fact, I'm back in my childhood home, with my best friend next door and playing varsity soccer. When I think back to my mom's idea of "new experiences," I can only marvel at how well her plan worked. And as for my crush? I saw her on my first day of senior year. She smiled, and I waved back.

From Anika's Essay "Wolfie the Wolf & Me":

> I thought the best part about playing with Wolfie was she was my baby, but now I know the best part was that I was happy. My journey has taught me to be strong, helped me rediscover my confidence, and provided me with lifelong friends. Some people might say I am unlucky because of my difference, but I

say I am lucky because I can tackle problems, honor sadness, and overall be filled with strength I never knew I had. I have learned a life lesson: plans don't always work out. I know I will pick up a child some day and hopefully fall in love, but until then I will take the lessons given me by my life's unexpected twist and keep learning.

As you think about how to close your essay, remember how each of these students connected theirs back to the SIDE DOOR ENTRANCE, with their first lines. This addition creates a narrative coherency that bathes the reader's brain in pleasing chemicals as we recognize the story we learned only minutes earlier and yet now we feel like old friends. Here's another fantastic introduction from Cooper's "The Outdoor Project." Based on his opening story, any guesses on how his essay ends? See its entirety in part III, chapter 13.

Excerpt from "The Outdoor Project"

The Marquam Trail slithers down from the top of Council Crest to the entrance of Oregon Health and Sciences University at 1,071 feet above Portland, Oregon. Locals in the Portland Heights neighborhood see it as a scenic hiking path, but thirteen-year-olds might consider it a great place for mountain-biking or to catch an adrenaline rush. The truth is that biking these trails is forbidden, but that's what makes it exciting. That's why most afternoons, I bounded off the bus, chucked my backpack in the corner, and grabbed the telephone to call up my best friend, Chucky D. The plan was the same everyday: meet me on Talbot Road behind your house. And instantly, we were screaming down the hard-packed, dirt trail, me on my aqua-blue Specialized Hard-Rock and him on his Mongoose-full-suspension bike, feeling the wind whipping around us, yanking all the worries from school away, and making us feel immortal.

A BACHELORS IN BRAINWORK

Bruce Ballenger, composition theorist and author of *The Curious Researcher*, says if your conclusion doesn't add something to your writing "cut it and try again." Such stern advice yet remembering the purpose of the conclusion helps us hear the wisdom in his words. While formal writing teaches us to restate thesis statements and main ideas, these ingredients are more like *functions* of the conclusion, yet the *purpose* of the final paragraph is more about showing perspective.

The conclusion is the place where you look backward and make sense of the knowledge you've gained. It's like saying "Hey, this whole examination of my topic was really valuable. In fact, I see connections that maybe I couldn't if I hadn't written them down." These new discoveries show up because the act of writing can actually provide perspective that's hard to find just by thinking or even talking. In other words, there's power in shaping your thoughts into language, and the conclusion is that place where you actually get to reach *conclusions* and make sense of your own extended inquiry.

Just like each essay is likely not your last piece of writing or your final conclusion, your ability to make sense of your life never ends. Outside of writing assignments or projects like the college application essay, where are you documenting insights about what you're learning about life? Where are you writing down your dreams, your plans, your goals?

If you don't already journal, I highly recommend finding a notebook that speaks to you, to track your observations about yourself and the world. Another benefit of recording your thoughts comes when you search them for patterns and recurring themes and begin to form your own conclusions.

Journaling is a technique many successful individuals use to track their goals, beliefs, and reflections. You can find countless online resources about the power of journaling to achieve things like weight loss goals or building better habits, but what I want to highlight speaks to the power of tracking your conclusions. What happens when we begin to observe patterns in our thinking to help us understand what we believe? Perhaps just as important as identifying your own beliefs is locating mistaken beliefs. These are the recurring thoughts limiting our effort or self-belief. Definitely watch out for ideas that rigidly inform you of your own poor possibilities. These, my friend, are not truths or beliefs to cling to, but thoughts to unlearn and rewrite with statements of purpose and possibility. How will you know when you've found one? Well, any thought referencing a hopeless future or an impossible pathway will certainly trigger the red flag—after all, you are young! There's plenty of time to become the person you want to be.

Drawing conclusions about your life is a wonderful practice to start as you enter college. Along with your favorite clothes and music, I hope you'll also bring a journal along with you next fall. You can find many topics to write about in the resource guide at writebig.net/resources.

"The difference between the *almost right* word
and the *right* word is really a large matter—
'tis the difference between the lightning bug and the lightning."
— Mark Twain

12

NEXT-LEVEL WRITING

A map for creating your essay is a big win—you now have a draft. It exists! But your college application essay can't be all it's meant to be if you don't commit to what I call "Next-Level Writing." If you've ever wondered about the difference between great and mediocre writing, or even the objective difference between an A and a B paper, it comes from some of the things you'll learn in this chapter. The qualities of "Next-Level Writing" are also a reason why so many students believe they're just not great writers. Students who struggle with writing may believe stronger writers apply these techniques to their writing naturally. And this belief may be partially true; in fact, students with a higher language aptitude may use "Next-Level Writing" techniques so much more than other students they even fool their teachers into thinking their writing is better than it is. Let's face it: teachers grade a lot of papers, so when teachers read the surprise and delights of strong word choice, diverse prose rhythm, and metaphor from some of their students, they recognize talent and perhaps even reward it with a grade. So, what's wrong with simply sounding smart?

If read carefully, that very same paper may be underdeveloped or even lack important content. This experience turned out to be my fate when I started college and tested out of the Introduction to College Writing class. I wrote well enough to surpass entry level expectations, but my writing process and my writing wasn't as mature as freshmen who'd taken college writing courses. So, when it was my turn to take second semester English, I filled my paper with the same flourishes that had wowed my high school English teacher. When my professor gave me a B-, I was stumped. What had I done wrong? Years later, I would be the professor and meet with many disgruntled freshmen convinced I was just a hard grader. When we reviewed their papers together, many came to see that their own ideas didn't always add up or make sense, despite unleashing a host of SAT vocabulary words. As students stuck with my teaching philosophy—to show them how to become better writers and give them skills to keep using and growing after my class—many students began to earn better grades naturally because they employed the techniques I taught throughout the course. And these are the same techniques I've been teaching you throughout *Write Big*.

Going through the process outlined in this book is much like taking my freshman English class. Actually, if you've followed the exercises in every chapter and looked at the examples, you've undoubtedly created a much better draft than the first paper I generally see from freshman college students. Why? Because it takes a whole semester for me to teach them everything included in *Write Big*. In a way, your college application essay represents something more like the *final* essay students write in my freshman class, where students are at what I call "the height of their powers" because they've spent a whole semester practicing writing. The week or two you've spent going through this book may have been an immersion experience in how to write well, but I don't want to just leave you with the draft you've created. I want to help you revise, edit, and polish it to perfection.

When my college students come to the end of a semester, I ask them to revise their work and apply all the lessons they've learned, but I also give them one more lesson about revision and editing, so they can turn in what I hope will be the best writing of their lives. And that's just what we want for your college application essay: to submit your best essay. Ever.

The following information comes from years of helping college freshmen become better writers but also years of helping upper division students write lovely personal narratives. I want you to have it all!

It's tempting to look at this chapter and think, "Wow, that's way too much work." You might have that reaction, but as you face those feelings I want you to remember a few things:

▶ You've worked hard to create meaningful content. Don't you want to ensure the image connects, the joke lands, or the punctuation succeeds?

▶ Much like the difference between an A and B paper, this important work will make a dramatic difference in the final outcome.

▶ Remember your goal. You want to be accepted into your top school; this essay won't be graded, but the degree to which it stands out, makes a great impression, and reflects who you are will be part of determining your future options.

What follows are ten Next-Level Writing tips to add flavor and music to your writing, a Subtraction Guide for cutting the right content to hit the 650-word count and sharpen your final draft, a Proofreading Checklist, and an Egregious Error Index.

I recommend you skim this chapter and note where you need the most changes. Then, move through each step within your essay.

TEN NEXT-LEVEL
WRITING TIPS

For your revision, we're going to focus on ten areas where you can have the most impact. These changes will be additions of high-value words and images, and sentence tinkering to give the reader an emotional experience, while also demonstrating strong writing skills.

1 Signposts. One of the most powerful tools in the revision process is rewriting the first sentence, sometimes the first two sentences of your paragraphs, for clarity, precision, and power. Think of it this way: if someone took out the first sentence of each of your paragraphs, you would want those sentences to read like the story of your essay. John Trimble, author of *Writing with Style*, calls these sentences "signposts," although you've likely learned them in school as topic sentences. In classrooms, teachers seem to understand their importance by requiring them in advance, along with thesis statements, but often struggle to convey just how important they are to create a smooth essay.

Here are the first lines, or signposts, from Matt's essay, "Grocery Lessons." Notice how, when read together, they create the skeleton of his essay.

> As I turned the wheel, I felt the lip of the curb hit my tires as I parked in the farthest empty spot from the grocery store.

> On a warm Saturday this September, I sat outside on my patio steps hoping to find anything to occupy my time.

> Apples: My first stop was the produce aisle.

> Coffee Creamer: My next stop was more complicated than my last.

Chicken: My final stop was the deli counter.

I clicked the button, the garage door opened, and I parked the car.

2 **Chain links:** Almost everyone knows it's best to have multiple paragraphs in an essay. Many of us understand a paragraph contains one main idea, developed with evidence and analysis. But few of us take the time to ensure our paragraphs connect to one another. In school, you may have learned to create a transition at the end of each paragraph, but as you become a more sophisticated writer, and as you need to write for a small word count, such as in the college application essay, you can begin to use the first line of each paragraph to create a linked chain. The first tip I discussed was signposts. I want to be clear that "signposts" and "chain links" are not two difference sentences, but rather you use your topic sentence to also double as a chain link. Imagine it's your job to link each paragraph to the next one. In its simplest form, we're talking about articulating the relationship between the main ideas in each paragraph. This important work is accomplished in two ways:

1) Using language, such as a repetition of a key word from the last sentence

2) Or, using a concept, such as hooking thoughts together based on the last sentence of one paragraph and the first of another. Here are some examples:

From Sarah's essay, "Date with Charlemagne":

> He could have dominated today's tabloids, yet the dust of time covered Charlemagne like a shroud. (Last line of NARRATIVE SITUATION 1)

> Before middle school, reading books had satisfied my fascination with history. (First line of NARRATIVE SITUATION 2)

In the above example, Sarah connects the two paragraphs, or creates a chain link, based on a concept: "Time covered Charlemagne like a shroud," which suggests the ancient past (Charlemagne is a historical figure and shroud is an old burial cloth) *and* "fascination with history," which names the subject that studies the ancient past.

Here's another example from the same essay, where Sarah hooks the paragraphs together with similar language:

> Teachers throughout the country incorporated my videos into their history curriculums, and even TED Talks referenced my endeavors. (Last line of STORY THREAD B)

> As educators repurposed my videos, I began to discover my own purpose. (First line of ADD IT UP)

In the above example, Sarah uses similar language (teacher/educator) to link together the next paragraph with the repetition of the root word purpose (repurposed/purpose). Using signposts to create chain links is what Trimble means when he names "a clean narrative line" as one of the hallmarks of a great essay.

3 **Comparisons:** Look for places where you can add a metaphor or analogy. These comparisons create images and give the reader another way to see your idea. In Sarah's essay, "Date with Charlemagne," examples such as "The dust of time covered Charlemagne like a shroud" or "This guy discarded more wives than a Hollywood leading man" are great examples. Warning: Don't use too many metaphors or analogies or beat your metaphors to death. Not everything is like something else. Also: Original metaphors can be tricky. Run your metaphors by a friend or two to make sure they make sense.

4 **Imagined Thoughts:** You can create drama by letting us know what was going through your head. See Davis's "A Ticket to Ride," when he writes, "I gave the driver a look that I hope said 'I have done this a million times.'" Along with specific detail, imagined thoughts are fantastic ways of

creating what in literature we call *verisimilitude*, meaning it helps the story resemble real life.

5 **Imagery:** These are word pictures that help your reader see the story. When E. B. White describes a thunderstorm by focusing on images like a "curious darkening of the sky" and the way the "boats suddenly swung the other way" in his essay "Once More to the Lake," we see these pictures in our mind. Here's an example from Cooper's "The Outdoor Project," where we really see him flying down the Marquam trail on his bike:

> And instantly, we were screaming down the hard-packed, dirt trail, me on my aqua-blue Specialized Hard-Rock and him on his Mongoose full-suspension bike, feeling the wind whipping around us, yanking all the worries from school away, and making us feel immortal.

6 **Humor:** Are you funny? Do you like to laugh? So does your reader. Having a light tone or using jokes or understatement is a fun way to showcase your intelligence. Oscar Wilde, the extremely witty playwright once said, "It is absurd to divide people into good and bad. People are either charming or tedious." This sort of observation isn't just funny it's somewhat philosophical. When it comes to humor, choose your jokes wisely. Make sure they show you in a good light, are not made at others' expense, and make someone smile or laugh.

Also, if you choose to use humor, don't surprise us at the end, but use humor throughout. See Davis's "Ticket to Ride," when he tells the story of his father dropping him off while he tries to return a pair of shoes:

> When I was about seven years old, my dad and I drove to downtown Portland to return a pair of hiking boots, except my dad was unable to find a parking spot. So, this meant I was to follow my father's instructions exactly, while he drove around the block: take the shoebox, walk into the store, and return to the person behind the counter. Unsurprisingly, there were

> complications with the return and the employee began to hurl
> questions at me. I panicked and bolted from the store through
> a blur of tears, leaving behind my desire for a new experience.

Davis's story is funnier because he does not explain the joke. It takes time to write something funny, but the trick writers like Davis use is something called *understatement.* Understatement is in contrast to sarcasm or a parenthetical statement like "I was such a goofball!" Important: Not every topic can be made humorous. Don't insert humor because it's on this list but because it works.

7 **Thematic language:** What emotion are you going for in your SIDE DOOR ENTRANCE? In your later paragraphs? Use language to help convey that emotion. Notice the effect this has in the introduction paragraph of "Ticket to Ride" and "Date with Charlemagne." In the first, we have words and phrases like: *fidget, jammed, jittery coins, a look that says I've done this a million times, the bus's pneumatic hiss, alone,* and *scuttled and stumbled as the bus jumped onto the road.* These words create a feeling of nervousness and uncertainty. In "Date with Charlemagne," the writer uses high-value words around the theme of adventure. She achieves this effect with words like: *raiding, crawling into the darkness, emerged to plunder, extract, dangerously-long, descended, unlatched the old costume chest,* and *raced back to the living room.*

8 **High-Value Language (Verbs and Nouns):** This lesson has two parts because it's so important. Let's look at verbs first.

VERBS: Every sentence has a verb so every sentence has an opportunity to create more action or emotion. Work to replace verbs with ones that consolidate the thought or action with ones that contain emotion, imagery, or precision. Notice the difference in meaning, intent, and emotion with the following verbs.

says	announce, repeats, confirms, debates
is	shows, demonstrates, highlights, illustrates
walks	strolls, wanders, skips, paces

For more high-value verbs, check out the resources I created to help readers of this book at writebig.net/resources.

PASSIVE VOICE: Passive Voice (PV) is a form of the verb "to be" plus the past participle or "-ed" form of verbs. It's not grammatically wrong, but it is stylistically boring and robotic. For the most part, you want to avoid it entirely. To fix passive voice:

First, run a search on your document for all forms of the verb "to be"—is, am, are, was, were, has been, had been, etc. Just finding a version of the verb "to be" won't mean you've discovered passive voice (but it may mean that you're overusing this verb), so you have to do the next step.

Then, if it's combined with an "-ed" verb or another irregular verb (for example: was burnt or has been shown), you want to correct it. The interesting part of correcting passive voice is the way it gives the whole sentence a face lift. Fix passive voice by identifying who or what is performing the action.

Passive Voice Makeovers

> *Meaning was imbued in all of Picasso's paintings.* (PV)

> Picasso imbued all of his work with meaning.

> *Blood was discovered at the crime scene.* (PV)

> Detectives discovered blood at the crime scene.

> *It was known in my school that Peter was the smartest kid in fifth grade.* (PV)

Everyone in my class knew that Peter was the smartest kid in fifth grade.

NOUNS: Novice writers often think adjectives (beautiful, glorious, azure, stunning) make sentences better, but powerful nouns are your friend, and when you have only 650 words you want to go to them first because they contain the concept and the lyricism we recognize in adjectives. Now, is also the time to replace vague or less interesting words with brighter, specific language. Again, start with your nouns.

Adjectives versus Nouns Examples

specific purpose	specificity
belligerent action	belligerence
glorious defeat	glory
beautiful morning	beauty

See Elijah's example from "Philosophy Talk." Notice the high-value nouns: pessimism, nihilism, existence, meaning, absurdism, condition, laughter, sunsets, randomness, satire, thirst:

> Pessimism should not be confused for nihilism. Pessimists perceive existence as emotional tragedy. Nihilists perceive existence as devoid of any intrinsic meaning. Absurdism adds a condition, saying: if there is no meaning, how can we value one meaningless thing over another? For Camus, this meant laughter and sunsets took precedent. For Harmon, this means pickle-people and alcoholism. For me, this means randomness, satire, and a thirst for knowledge. How does Harmon channel his absurdism? Let's take a look into the chaotic world of Rick and Morty.

9 Prose Rhythm: Rhythm is a musical term, but it also applies to how your writing sounds to the reader. The other additions I recommended will help you add vibrancy to your writing, but prose rhythm will go a step further by enhancing your thoughts with a focus on sentence variety. Trimble instructs to create a strong prose rhythm by writing three long sentences, followed by a short sentence. The reverse is also true. Keep in mind that short sentences back-to-back create a breathless quality, perfect for action sequences or intentional revelation of quick thoughts *but* not quite right for most else. Finally, medium-length sentences throughout your writing create a boring and mechanical sound, much like a manual or dictionary. If you're looking to make some final improvements, spend time on prose rhythm. Here's an example from Stephanie's "The Lego Story," that showcases the lovely sentence variety of prose rhythm:

> Take the man in the restaurant, about to propose. Strip away his shiny ring. Bring him outside the building, on his knees, arms outstretched. Now he is a beggar, holding out a plastic cup in hopes someone will donate to the cause. Or, move him up several stories, above the restaurant, into the apartment. Here he creates masterpieces of artwork, which are sold all over town. One even hangs in the mayor's office. Through what some would call play, I learned innovation, creativity, and just a little bit of rule breaking—because when I changed the job or position of the characters, I went against the rulebook that demanded they stay put.

Notice how she begins the first three sentences with commands—take, strip, bring—all medium-short length sentences. Then, she adds the fourth sentence, a longer statement. She repeats these choppy commands and explanations and then ends with a longer, fluid sentence that brings together the meaning.

10 Lists: Lists are almost in the subtraction category (explained in greater detail next), because they allow you to consolidate information. They also help you to layer thoughts and images in stylistic succession, which adds interest and variety. Lists are extremely handy in the college application essay because they pack content into paragraphs by either listing facts or images. They're also crucial to the ADD IT UP paragraph, where you want to showcase other accomplishments and experiences that connect with your SIDE DOOR ENTRANCE.

See Ellie's list from "With and Without You," where she explains how being a twin has shaped her world view:

> Today I use my "twinness" to help the important people in my life: tutoring my friends in math and science, comforting my younger and homesick cousin who moved from Indonesia to the United States, and volunteering at a therapeutic barn for kids with special needs. This genuine compassion for the wellbeing of others is an important lens that I use to see the world.

THE SUBTRACTION GUIDE

Subtraction is not just about cutting out content to achieve a specific word count, but about making your writing sharp and compelling. Hopefully, in your additions you also made subtractions as you altered verbs, nouns, and created prose rhythm. At this point, you might have more than 650 words. If you are like most of my students, you may even have one hundred to three hundred words too many. So where do you make cuts?

For making cuts, try the funnel approach, beginning with the biggest cuts first.

1 **Look for tangents.** Tangents are places in your essay where you offer a story, explanation, or detail that is off-topic or doesn't fit within the main idea of the paragraph. Tangents may be whole paragraphs or partial paragraphs, so look for both. Cut these first. Ask yourself: Is this great writing but doesn't work here? Or, is this writing helpful but not essential? When I say essential, I don't mean cutting your images or metaphor or description. It's essential to give your reader an emotional experience. Nonessential information might be a second sentence of explanation that could be blended into one or a thought that could be extracted without harming the meaning. Be tough. You want to find the tangent yourself and cut it, not the admissions counselor.

2 **Search for repetition.** Are there whole sentences or groups of sentences that repeat an earlier idea or are no longer relevant? Cut these first. Then move on to cutting words. If you know you have pet words you use often, run a search for these words.

3 **Word Consolidation:** Look for places where you can consolidate your phrasing with a powerful verb or noun.

4 **Wasted Words.** Look for words that don't advance the meaning. Adverbs can often be cut—*really, especially, absolutely*—but also nonessential words such as:

> for me
>
> in my opinion
>
> like
>
> that

5 **Hyphenate Words.** Use hyphens when appropriate. Saying I was a nine-year-old girl counts as one word in the word count as does self-reflective. Be careful, however, because not every word can be hyphenated. Hyphenating age is a tricky business, as the phrase 'nine year old' is not

hyphenated because it does not modify a noun. To ensure correctness, consult a hyphen guide in your final proofread.

Sometimes it's easier for someone else to cut words for you. But be careful what they cut! Remember to save your original draft and advise them to avoid seeing your literary flourishes as fluff to be eliminated.

When should you invite readers into your draft?

I strongly recommend *not* sharing your draft with parents, teachers, or peers, in order to receive help with corrections until you've finished chapter 12. Receiving competing advice, which is what happens when you have multiple readers, is often counter-productive to creating a stellar first draft.

However, when you are ready, please be sure when taking grammatical advice, you are asking an expert, such as your English teacher or a writing professional. Peers and parents (sorry parents, but it's true) often do not understand the goals of the college application essay and therefore provide contrary feedback to the storytelling approach or even offer wrong editing corrections.

If you are a grammatical wizard yourself—awesome! But please still have a someone else read your final essay. Even I, a professional writer and writing teacher, have an editor for my book.

 PROOFREADING CHECKLIST

Proofreading is the final step to ensure you create the right impression. No one wants to be remembered for silly errors or for their run-on sentences. Follow this checklist to ensure you've covered these final details.

✓ **Read** your draft aloud each time you proofread. Before you click submit, you should have read your essay at least three times aloud and found no mistakes. Printing your draft is best.

✓ **If you fix a mistake,** you must read the whole essay over again. Why? Because every time you touch your draft, you introduce the possibility for errors. You want your essay to be error free.

✓ **Commas.** Look for run-ons, sentence fragments, and places that need commas for clarification. How do you know if they're correct? There are whole chapters in grammar books on commas, but I recommend you review the following four comma rules and apply these to your college application essay as you proofread.

1. **Coordinating conjunction** plus comma. Omitting the comma with this rule is the comma error I see the most. Independent clauses joined by a coordinating conjunction—and, but, for, nor, so, and yet—are always separated by a comma and then the joining word.

Last year, Alli was accepted to Harvard, but she decided to attend Columbia.

2. **Nonessential clauses.** Use commas like parenthesis when you're adding optional information into the sentence.

Emory University is in Atlanta, my birthplace.

The University of Oregon accepts many Northwest students, notably college-bound seniors from Oregon, into the Clark Honors College.

3. **Introductory clause** plus comma. In general, add a comma after an introductory clause.

In the fall of senior year, 80 percent of American high school students will complete at least one college application.

4. **The Oxford comma.** This comma rule is considered stylistic, meaning it's not required; however, many humanities disciplines prefer it. The controversial Oxford comma is the last comma in a series.

Katherine applied to all prestigious colleges around the country like Princeton, Stanford, and Berkley.

✓ **Semicolons.** Semicolons are flashy grammar. If you're not 100 percent certain of semi-colon usage, then you either want to look it up or not use it. The golden rule here is that semicolons can never, ever, ever be interchanged with a comma. So that means you just can't decide to add one. What are they used for?

1. **Joining independent clauses.** In this instance, the semicolon implies relationship between the two ideas.

Semicolons can save words on your college application essay; they also make you look smart.

2. When using the words *however, moreover,* and *therefore* (among others) as **conjunctive adverbs.**

Conjunctive adverbial clause is such a stuffy phrase; however, once you memorize it you can impress your friends.

3. As a **super comma.** Semicolons can be used to separate independent clauses into a list. This usage is probably their most sophisticated and impressive.

Semicolons separate independent clauses; this impressive punctuation is required for adverbial clauses; they can even be used a super comma.

EGREGIOUS ERRORS INDEX

APOSTROPHES: Check all for correctness.

PROPER NOUN CAPITALIZATION: Academic subjects are not capitalized unless they're part of titles or names of courses. Besides the obvious capitalizations of names of people and places, refresh your capitalization knowledge when proofreading your final copy.
Samson will study mathematics at the University of Oregon.
He will be taking courses such as Computational Mathematics in his freshmen year.

SUBJECT/VERB AGREEMENT:

Nico, along with his friends, swims every Saturday afternoon is **correct**.
Nico, along with his friends, swim every Saturday afternoon is **incorrect**.

PLURALIZATION VS. POSSESSIVE: Our family's vacation vs families vacation at the beach

VAGUE PRONOUN REFERENCE, i.e. *this, that, it*

WRONG WORD: Look up any uncertain words. The college application essay is not a great place to try out new vocabulary words unless you've read or heard someone speak them in a sentence. However, using a thesaurus is a great tool to remind you of words you already know.

MISSING WORD: Reading your work aloud will help you catch missing/repeated words.

MECHANICAL ERROR WITH QUOTATION MARKS:
In "Philosophy Talk" Elijah writes about absurdism is incorrect because the comma should precede the quotation marks. *In "Philosophy Talk," Elijah writes about absurdism* is correct.

Run a check on your document for your own personal foibles. For example, check for all forms of the word they're/their/there if this trips you up. Triple check to be sure you're using these homonyms and near-homonyms correctly.

> They're/their/there
> Its/it's
> To/too/two
> Effect/affect
> Definitely/defiantly
> Bare/bear
> Your/You're
> Than/Then
> Through/Threw
> Sees/Seas/Seize

As you finish up part II of *Write Big*, remember the time and effort spent will make a noticeable difference in your essay. All of the student examples in this book went through multiple drafts, editing, and polishing before they were ready for admissions counselors. Here's one more excerpt from another excellent essay as inspiration to keep working on your draft. Ellie's "With and Without You" is an insightful and heartbreaking narrative that explores losing her twin sister when she was five years old. You can read all of Ellie's powerful essay in part III, chapter 13.

Excerpt from "With and Without You"

When Merav, my twin sister, was feeling healthy, I knew I was going to have a good day. On these days, Merav would support herself on the kitchen island, opening all the cabinets as she went along in the circle. The pattern was always the same. She opened seven cabinets with a creak, and I followed her, closing them with a thud. We would repeat this for hours. It always put a smile on her face, which put a smile on my face too.

Merav was born with a rare, spontaneous genetic disorder in which her brain was too small. She had trouble processing and sending information to her body because her brain did not fully develop. Due to this anomaly, parts of her brain would shut off causing her to have atonic, clonic, and grand mal seizures. As a child, my most vivid memories include Merav's seizures: the way she would stare off into space, as if she wasn't even there; the way her arms and legs would fall asleep; and the way her whole body would twitch. When Merav died at five-years-old, due to her heart stopping, I wondered what the world would be like without her.

A BACHELORS IN BRAINWORK

Revision is a word that's unfortunately associated with the *redo* concept, which also means it's associated with extra work or work that no one loves doing. But let's see if I can get you to think of it in a different way. In my college classes I loved writing the word on the board like this:

Re   *Vision*

If we look at the individual roots of this word, we see something more:

RE: Again

VISION: See.

In fact, just this exercise is a kind of revision—to see a word again. And it's exactly what readers do with literary analysis, to consider the layers of meaning in just one word.

In writing, the capacity to *see* your work *again* has enormous implications. If you give your writing a rest, say a day or two, and return to it later, the ability to see it with new eyes means the capacity to not only locate mistakes but to reimagine possibilities, to further explore, and to ultimately make it better.

While revision is often used to discuss plans and documents, what happens when we extend the concept of *see again* to our lives? Now I don't mean the kind of thing where we have a fight with a friend, and then we replay the conversation over and over again in our heads. But instead, what happens when we look at our lives not just critically but with imagination? What happens when we say to ourselves "Yes, I'm heading this way. But is there another way that's better? Is there more than one way?"

Like the previous chapter when I discussed the way life conclusions can be both helpful and limiting, revision is also a story tool to help us articulate the life we want—perhaps even before it's happened.

148

In fact, psychologists like Daniel Siegel, author of *The Developing Mind*, consider this ability—the capacity to tell your story with meaning—as something called a *coherent life narrative*. And what's more, those who've created a coherent life narrative have the ability to overcome the past challenges of their lives because they've done the work of making sense of the pain, loss, and obstacles in their upbringing. If you read all of Ellie's "With and Without You," in part III, you'll see an insightful young woman doing just that: making sense of her loss and how she's been shaped by it. She makes surprising insights about the way her "twinness" helps her move in the world, even while her twin is no longer with her.

Unlike a simple edit, where we exchange a mistake for correction, revising our story means retelling it in a way that makes sense, thus the *coherency* in the phrase *coherent life narrative*. Writing theorist and journalist Donald Murray, author of *The Craft of Revision*, defines revision this way, "Revision is the reordering of experience so that it reveals meaning." If you use the simple tool of *see again*, just on Murray's quote, what do you notice about his definition of revision now? Which words stand out to you? If you noticed words like "experience," "reveal," and "meaning," you're on the track to discovering how revising your writing, or your life, means to use both analysis and imagination.

As you polish off your college application essay, I encourage you to notice the way you've made sense of an aspect of your life, your topic. As you've done so, consider if there are any other areas of your life that could benefit by integrating them into your story, in order to give you the power of coherency. That doesn't mean to include them in the essay, but rather to consider how just writing this essay provides insight into who you are, and hopefully where you want to go next.

To practice creating a "working" life narrative to guide you through your college journey, visit the resource guide at <u>writebig.net/resources</u>.

PART III:
HEROIC TALES FROM COLLEGE-BOUND SENIORS

"A person who has good thoughts cannot ever be ugly. You can have a wonky nose and a crooked mouth and a double chin and stick-out teeth, but if you have good thoughts they will shine out of your face like sunbeams and you will always look lovely."
— Roald Dahl, *The Twits*

13

ORIGIN STORIES

Katherine

Katherine studies political science at George Fox University in the William Penn Honors Program, where she receives $18,000 annually in scholarships, including the school's Presidential Award. Her devotion to political issues began at home with a family legacy that includes a commitment to social justice. She completed an extended service trip to Kampala, Africa as a middle-school student and today works toward solutions for refugee resettlement. Katherine serves as a cultural ambassador for GFU and extends her multicultural interests by working in Turkish textiles while in college. She recently completed a semester abroad in Prague, where she studied at Charles University. Katherine's essay is a unique twist on the Common Application's backstory prompt, as she explores the unshakeable distinction of growing up as the oldest in her family. Many students associate this prompt with hardship and tragedy, yet Katherine shows how college-bound seniors can write a remarkable essay about the positive forces that shape our lives.

WENDY AND THE LOST BOYS

We were sitting in the hall, propped up against our lockers when Caroline studied me and said, "Katherine, if you were a Disney character, you'd be Wendy." My first thought was, really, she's not even a princess? As I quickly ran through the list of Disney beauties before first period, I realized her comparison was startlingly accurate.

As children, Peter Pan's captivating sense of mystery and freedom entices us, but few stop to realize that the key to his whimsical success is his practical partner Wendy. For as long as I can remember, I have been an older sister. I was only eighteen months old when the first of three younger brothers was born. My brothers' names are Jack, Peter, and Matthew, and they have become the Lost Boys to my Wendy. In J.M Barrie's classic tale, Peter is the one fighting imaginary pirates, while Wendy is the one looking after The Lost Boys. Wendy is the calming presence that holds this band of rambunctious boys together.

Until I left homeschool for public school in the fourth grade, I lived in a kind of Neverland with my brothers. Homeschool was like the feeling of coloring outside of the lines: lessons at the kitchen table, the outdoor Greek Olympics, homemade documentaries, mud castles, buried treasure, worms, leaves, insects, and most importantly, our backyard. In the backyard our imagination was allowed to run wild and we were our own masters. In the midst of this creative freedom, it was my job to keep everyone together. Whether we were in the treehouse or the sandbox, I made sure no one was left behind. As I grew up, being a sister started to look different. When winter came, it meant helping little fingers find their way into gloves or hunting down missing rain boots. When it was time to go to public school, it meant helping mom pack lunches or herding younger siblings towards the car. In high school, it has meant dropping boys off for practice and often times fetching forgotten shin-guards or soccer balls. Being an older sister has been exciting, challenging, tiring, rewarding, frustrating, and an amazing learning experience.

I'd like to think that I'm helping to mold these young men as they grow up, but the truth is that they are molding me. Being their older sister has taught me how to be a patient and nurturing leader, as well as a supportive friend and a team player. Just this fall I was a passenger in my own car for the first time because Jack got his license. Now it takes twenty minutes to get to school instead of fifteen, and I try to stay calm as he negotiates the clutch, but this also means more time in the car with one of my best friends.

Perhaps most importantly, the boys have taught me the significance of others. Although it may be you wiping peanut butter and jelly off their faces, you need them as much as they need you. After an exhausting cross-country practice last night, Pete came into my room to study and then hung around afterwards to flip through my collection of vintage magazines. Sometimes, when I'm stepping on legos strewn across the floor, or folding laundry that isn't mine, I wonder what it would be like to be the youngest. What would it be like to have other people drop me off or make my lunch? What I've realized is that it's not about being the youngest or the oldest, but about being a member of a team. As an older sister I've learned not only how to take care of others, but how to take care of myself too. I may not be a Cinderella, or a Sleeping Beauty, but I now see the importance of being a Wendy character.

Thea

Thea is a 2018 National Merit Scholarship finalist, with big plans to study astronomy and physics in college. Due to her National Merit attention, she received full-ride offers from colleges, including Seattle University and Arizona State University. With acceptances and scholarship offers into Rice University and Macalester College, Thea ultimately chose Wellesley College, the prestigious all-women's school outside of Boston. In addition to her stellar school performance, semester abroad in Germany, and leadership positions in high school, Thea has an active YouTube channel where she posts music gaming videos, some with over 150,000 views! She is an avid reader and ice skater, and according to her mom Margret, a fantastic cook. Thea plans to continue in the field of astrophysics after earning her undergraduate degree. "Math Matters" offers us a wonderful example of how to write about complex subjects like mathematics. Because Thea's academic record clearly shows her strengths in math and science, her conversational writing ability also gives admissions readers a window into this talented and well-rounded student.

MATH MATTERS

The story begins with a train. It may be an Intercity-Express from Stuttgart, or a Train à Grande Vitesse from Paris, but it's always a train. And on that train, two kids play catch: one of the them winds up, prepares to throw, and yet, doesn't move. He, like everything else on the train, is perfectly still. The twist? The train is moving near light-speed, when time itself seems to stop.

That was the kind of bedtime story I grew up with--while other children rode dragons and spaceships, my father and I booked passage on lightspeed trains to learn about relativity. The way I see it, I grew up submerged in two languages: German and math. From my father, who wrote his doctorate on representation theory, I gained fluency in mathematics, and from my mother, a clinical pathologist who grew up in Aalen, a small town in Germany, I heard only Deutsch.

Both parents form my weltanschauung (literally, how I see the world). For example, years after I fell asleep to those bedtime stories, I lay in a dark hotel room with my best friend in the bed next to mine. She was going off to college and was terrified she would be lonely there. I, in my infinite wisdom, explained, "Statistically speaking, it's highly improbable that will be the case." Then I did some math: if she could find at least one friend in a population as small as Riverdale High School (n = 246), she would likely be able to find one in a population ten times larger (n = 2600). Thankfully, she thought I was funny rather than heartless, but the point stands.

Life's a little bit like math: no one gets it all the first time around. The first time I discovered the concept of time dilation, it made absolutely no sense. It took many walks to Starbucks with my dad for things to click. Years later, when I first cracked open a book on combinatorics, I understood exactly none of it. It was only months later, when I participated in a math retreat in the Schwarzwald dedicated to the subject, that things finally began to add up.

As a rule, the first time you face some mathematical concept, there's a high probability that you won't understand it. In order to understand said concept, you have to keep at it, and doing so means putting up with this incomprehension. And so from math I learned resilience. I learned to live with discomfort, and more importantly, I learned the necessity of this tolerance. This doesn't just apply to math. Knowing that I can tolerate discomfort gives me the confidence to push myself and explore outside of my comfort zone, like when I spent a semester at a boarding school in Germany. Ultimately, I know that I have the resilience to survive it.

Math taught me something else, as well: everything is connected. The language of math has allowed me to pursue my interest in astrophysics, like with the train. In my physics class in Germany, for example, I used Stokes' Theorem to understand the Maxwell Equations, but it goes beyond STEM too. My experience with mathematics has given me practice in looking for patterns and connections, which comes in handy when writing essays. I don't see my classes as individual units; instead, they combine into a larger whole, where the sum of the products is greater than each single class on its own.

On nights when my mom was in charge of bedtime, we had a different tradition. Instead of taking hyper-fast trains, we'd go on a tour of the digestive tract. We started with the mouth and followed a piece of food through the body, passing a new organ each night. And if we didn't make it all the way through in a night, that was okay. There was always tomorrow.

Madeline

After receiving acceptances from the University of San Francisco, Seattle, Clark, and Fordham Universities, Madeline chose to study at Brandeis University in Waltham, Massachusetts. She is earning an interdisciplinary degree in labor and employment policy, from the prestigious university. With a passion for social justice, Madeline's found a home as the coordinator for the Brandeis Labor Coalition and as an intern with WATCH, an organization in Waltham that works to diminish housing insecurity in the community. And with a background in dance and performance, she's joined the West African Drumming and Dancing Club, as well as the Brandeis Swingers. She plans to study abroad in Buenos Aires, Argentina with the program Social Movements and Human Rights during her junior year. Additionally, Madeline will be in Portland in the summer of 2018 working with oral histories with the Pacific Northwest Labor History Association. She notes that after all the hard work of applying to colleges in exciting cities and faraway places, college has helped shaped an appreciation for her life back in Oregon. Her unique upbringing on a rural farm co-op provided her with surprising worldly insights, integrated within her college application essay below. Her farm-work ethic not only showcases her familiarity with a rigorous lifestyle but also highlights her awareness of this helpful training for a future in college and beyond.

FARM SKILLS ARE LIFE SKILLS

Madeline versus the hoof: my weekly challenge. If I'm not vigilant at 7:30am on Sundays, while milking our moody goat PJ, a stray hoof may spoil the day's earnings. When I pinch her warm freckled, udders between my thumb and fingers, a light sprinkling of milk ricochets off the pail. PJ's left back leg twitches, telling me it's time to fill her bowl with another scoop of grain to keep her occupied. Only four years ago I witnessed PJ's fragile birth, lifting her small body as she learned how to use her skinny legs. Now that leg, not so skinny any more, threatens me, dictating the exact ratio of passion to pressure required for a single pail of milk.

Milking PJ represents an important lesson of farm life: sometimes you put your knees into the dirt and work. Every task is shared on Wingspan Farm, the community of three families that I've called home for the last nine years, yet there is never a lack of work to be done. Most springs I spend weeding garden beds and feeding animals, but when August comes it's time to dig into the soil for the treasure of golden potatoes, to pull dripping frames from the beehive, and to eat a tortilla filled with rich goat meat, fresh tomatoes, and crumbled feta. Then, every drop of sweat is worth it.

Work on the farm has prepared me for other areas of my life: I attend a Japanese charter school, where the stress of complex group projects with students of all ages is constant and the difficulty of learning an Eastern Language is a daily challenge. But, as with the rewards on the farm, I wouldn't have it any other way. Each complicated endeavor is also a benefit, such as the freedom to research, choreograph, and perform modern dance in the influential style of Martha Graham.

Life on a small farm has given me a perspective on a large world. I have shared the chores like milking, feeding, and cutting hooves, while developing the skills of a stellar team member because one can never make a decision independently when living in community. I have been part of countless farm meetings, deciding everything from how much asparagus to plant, to who will lead the goats to their death on the day of slaughter.

Last year I used these collaborative skills on a trip to Mexico with my family. Wandering the colorful stalls of a Oaxacan market we met Lourdes, a bright, energetic woman responsible for educating her community to be increasingly sustainable and consequently less hungry. Many in her community feared using their many wandering goats for milk and cheese. My parents and I created a partnership with Lourdes to help her community understand the value of their resources. We sent photos of us, Americans, straining and drinking our goat milk, to assuage their fears. This opportunity taught me the importance of education and collaboration in creatively solving world problems, a topic incredibly important to me.

In Mexico, I helped teach a new generation how to use the resources around them; this August it'll be time to teach the next generation in my community. August at Wingspan Farm means Farm Camp, a time to gather together with youngsters waiting excitedly to squeeze the warm milk from PJ's udders. Their small hands will barely produce a teaspoon of milk, but the joy that appears on their faces would bubble over the rim of any pail. After battling PJ's naughty hoof, they will stand around the dining room table drinking the warm, foamy fruits of their labor. Before they go, I leave them with something important to think about: this milk is the product of hard work, collaboration and passion, and they, like me, are very lucky because not everyone has opportunities like this.

Jack

After years of living abroad, Jack moved back to his home state of Oregon, researched and applied to colleges in and out of state, and ultimately chose to stick around the Northwest. An ambitious and gregarious student, Jack knew he wanted a large university with school spirit, which made his ultimate pick, the University of Oregon, a top selection. He plans to study either business or political science at U of O and sees himself pursuing law school or graduate programs afterward. Jack says he can't wait to meet new people and build relationships in college; his parents say Jack values community and believe he will thrive in a bustling college setting. His funny and insightful essay about his experiences living in China illustrates how to write about elusive concepts like cultural awareness. Like many writers, Jack knew the meaning of his experience but struggled to show how he'd arrived at a greater understanding of valuing cultural differences. The revisions to his SIDE DOOR ENTRANCE, NARRATIVE SITUATION, and STORY THREAD paragraphs work together to bring the reader into his experiences abroad and reveal the lessons that fostered Jack's maturity and personal growth while living internationally.

LIVE CHICKEN

It's been a long time since I've seen the photograph of me holding a live chicken at the marketplace in Guilin, China. But even as I imagine it, I feel the blood rushing to my face, as a tiny, wrinkled Chinese woman shoves a flustered hen at me, while I struggle to steady my trembling hands. I see my mom fumble for her phone, and through a clenched smile I plead, "Quick mom, quick!" Cheese. Click. Flash. The old Chinese ladies howl with laughter, and mom gets the shot.

When I was ten years old, my parents told me we were moving to China. At the time, I didn't even like rice. We didn't move because of a job transfer or in political protest, but because my parents wanted to give us, in my mom's words "a new experience." But who needs new experiences when my best friend lives behind my backyard gate, my soccer team just won state, and the girl I have a crush on likes me back. As a fourth grader, my objections were overruled: I would be starting 5th grade in Shekou International School.

At the Guilin marketplace, we were not only far from Portland, Oregon but far from Shekou. While Shekou is a quick-growing city near Hong Kong, Guilin is a small farming village in the countryside, abundant with picturesque karst hills and rice paddies. The wet-market was the place where Guilin villagers sold their items: fresh vegetables, small fish, bundles of rice, and animals, both dead and alive. If nothing else, my time in China showed me the value of embracing both chaos, and simplicity, because both turn you into a stronger person.

Dealing with chaos became a way of life during the seven years my family lived and traveled abroad. One of our first tastes of seeming anarchy came from the marketplace, where we observed sickly people being "leeched," the hanging heads of alligators and bulls, and hundreds of villagers darting around with food in their mouths. Don't even get me started on the stench of fish looming in the air. I looked up at my parents, back to the alligator heads, and wondered "what am I doing here?" However, to my surprise, the longer I lived in China, the more comfortable I became with situations just like this. Years later when I found myself in New Delhi, India on a soccer trip, I noticed my teammates' astonishment at the lack of driving rules, as we sped past a fallen motorcyclist, and later as we stopped along with hundreds of cars for a cow to cross the road.

The counter to chaos is perhaps simplicity, also part of everyday life in China. I enjoyed the old rusty bikes that whizzed past and bartering with street vendors for noodles. However, when simplicity was presented as restricted access to browse the internet or visit the doctor, I wondered if the government feared its citizens access to westernized freedoms. I learned this firsthand when I crossed the Chinese border for medical treatment, due to an allergic reaction to my HPV vaccine. This experience helped me gain an appreciation for people like the Guilin locals covered with leeches; not everyone has access to western medicine, yet they still manage to live healthy lifestyles.

Much has changed since that first day in the Guilin marketplace. My family no longer lives in China, or in Dubai (which is where we lived post-Shekou), or treks the globe to places like France, the Philippines, or Oman. In fact, I'm back in my childhood home, with my best friend next door and playing varsity soccer. When I think back to my mom's idea of 'new experiences,' I can only marvel at how well her plan worked. And as for my crush? I saw her on my first day of senior year. She smiled, and I waved back.

Gillian

Gillian began her college career at Pacific Lutheran University in Tacoma, Washington as a music major but fell in love with writing junior year in her general education course. A recipient of the Knudsen Family Memorial Scholarship for Creative Writing and the Chester Buhl Music Scholarship, Gillian redesigned her studies to graduate with degrees in English literature, writing, and music. She has already been published in the Dorset Fiction Award Anthology, and after graduation, Gillian looks forward to teaching English abroad and finishing up her studio album. Her poignant college application essay explores themes of individual and collective identity, as she recounts her personal history with sharing a birthday with a national tragedy.

BORN ON SEPTEMBER 11TH

My fifth birthday was important. This is not chiefly because it was my *birthday*, nor because my mother had made my kindergarten class homemade cupcakes the night before. No, the significance of that specific birthday is due to the fact that I was born on September 11th, 1996. Five years later to the day, perspectives, world-views, and lives changed for millions of Americans. Meanwhile, a five-year-old girl sat at a dining room table in Portland, Oregon and blew out candles on a cake.

"I'm so sorry." This is not the response a six-year-old is expecting when she tells her first grade class that it is her special day. I would hastily reply to these comments with the answer that my mother gave me: "Good things can happen on bad days." But innocence in the face of tragedy bypassed the emotional sensitivity the day required, and so for the years to follow my family avoided celebrating my happiest day with the rest of the world, by changing party dates and delaying gifts. *How dare they take the day away?* I wanted cupcakes. I wanted my birthday to be all mine. In my eyes, September 11th's connotation and shorthand for American mourning had taken my birthday away from me. It would be a while before I came to understand that sharing is not always about losing a piece, but about connecting to a greater picture.

I made my discovery on my fourteenth birthday. For the first time, I looked up the live footage of the twin towers going down and subsequently spent hours plugged into my computer. I scrolled through Wikipedia pages and searched for the information I had subconsciously avoided. Two towers, three planes, and nearly three thousand people had died. That night, over thirty kids ran around my backyard, played loud music, and wished me a happy birthday. It was as if nothing had happened nine years ago. I realized that night as I laughed with my friends, on the first real birthday celebration I'd had since I was five, that my identity exists in the space between the destruction of the towers and who I am today.

On the tenth anniversary of 9/11, I turned fifteen. The tradition at my school is to begin the day with a morning prayer and to announce student birthdays. On this day, the loudspeaker came on: "We request a call to silence in memory of the lives lost ten years ago." Heads bowed and the smirks and giggles that normally accompany the morning prayer were absent. A minute passed and the voice returned. "Thank you. And happy birthday to class of '14, Gillian Dockins."

"There are gifts in everything." My mother, a wise sage with silver hair has raised me to believe this deeply. I'm still not exactly sure what to say when people ask me what it is like to share my birthday with a national tragedy; sometimes it feels like the most trivial piece of my identity, and sometimes it seems that it defines me to the core. We choose what makes us who we are, and for what it's worth, I will always choose my birthday. In the end, we live with both joy and sadness-- they are balancing and they are strengthening, not opposites, but intertwined.

Cade

Cade studies civil engineering at Oregon State University's nationally recognized College of Engineering, in Corvallis. He participates in the university's Multiple Engineering Co-op Program (MECOP) that matches engineering students with business internships. Cade is the proud recipient of the Howard Vollum American Indian Scholarship, as well the Finley Academic Excellence Scholarship. He is also a member of OSU's chapter of Sigma Phi Epsilon and recently received the organization's Balanced Man scholarship. Fraternity life was just the next step for Cade, as you will see from his college application essay, which explores the advantages of growing up in a blended family with seven boys.

FAMILY TIES

Spring break was among us. Everyone was leaving their cold Portland, Oregon homes for someplace warmer. For my family, that meant a sixteen-hour drive from Portland to Palm Springs, California. This was my first road trip with my recently acquainted stepbrothers, and there was no telling how this car ride would play out. I strategically sat next to the van's right sliding door, the car's best escape route. Six hours in, I was sweating profusely and counting down the hours, until I escaped this hot metal deathtrap. There were arguments over the radio. There were arguments over the snacks. There were arguments over which way the AC blew. Soon, I heard my youngest stepbrother, wedged in the backseat, squeal for a bathroom break. Only five minutes had passed, since the last "emergency" stop. We stopped at the closest gas station, piling out one by one, and a few minutes later, we piled right back in. I was certain someone was going to crack.

My family isn't the average size. With 7 boys total, with myself exactly in the middle, it can be a hectic place. Only a few months before that car ride, I'd had only one brother, and we'd struggled to get along. With such a large family, I wondered how it would all work. And like most children, I was a tad self-centered. Now almost eight years later, I can say I've discovered the wisdom in working together and the value of fending for myself.

My cooperation and flexibility were not polished over a sixteen-hour drive but more like a couple of years. In my new family setting, rather than a "yours and mine" policy that had worked with just my brother and me, I had to be open to change. One of the first things to go was my individual toothpaste, which soon became shared amongst multiple siblings. I had to adjust to the harsh mistreatment of my toothpaste, the squashed tube now smothered in germs. I learned to let it go. Around this same time, I transferred into a new school district, which also meant a new basketball team. The recent relationships skills I gained came in handy as I developed good chemistry with my team in only a short time.

Not only did I learn to get along with others, I also realized the relationship between independence and confidence. With my parents' hands full, I had to learn to solve my own problems. Later, when I started my summer job at QFC grocery store, my manager was often unavailable to help me. When the can machine for bottle recycling broke, the customers were often grumpy, and I was on my own to troubleshoot effectively. Through trial and error, I diagnosed the machine, got it working again, and handed it back to the pacified customers. As I look back, I feel lucky that my parents were not always there to help me. Remembering the road trip, I thought independence meant having my own way, but now I know that figuring things out on my own is its own reward.

When we arrived at our rental house in Palm Springs, the only person who cracked was my step dad. But that's what sixteen hours, ten stops, and seven boys will do to you. In the end, however, the road trip was a sign that we could learn to live together as one big family. More than that, I grew from the self-focused kid that I once was to the cooperative and capable young adult that I'm proud to be today.

Cooper

When Cooper received admission into his first-choice university, he was delighted. However, when his acceptance to St. Mary's College of California included a letter from the dean of admissions who applauded the way Cooper's essay made him experience the snow of Heather Canyon, he knew all of the revisions of his Common Application Essay had indeed been worth it. Throughout high school, Cooper worked hard to overcome the challenges of disability and his acceptance into St. Mary's, one of only forty-four schools featured in Loren Pope's book *Colleges That Change Lives* and also ranked in the Top Ten Universities in the West by U.S. News and World Report, was a celebration of his perseverance. The dean's letter also included sizable awards, with an annual $17,000 Benildus Merit Scholarship and a $10,000 Alumni Scholarship. Cooper notes that acceptance into his top school was really just a first step. He reminds aspiring college students that freshman year is harder than you think, "It's not all just one big party," he says. In his essay, Cooper shows St Mary's the origin of his hard-work ethic as he recounts the history of overcoming disability to achieve success in school—especially when he'd rather be outside.

THE OUTDOOR PROJECT

The Marquam Trail slithers down from the top of Council Crest to the entrance of Oregon Health and Sciences University at 1,071 feet above Portland, Oregon. Locals in the Portland Heights neighborhood see it as a scenic hiking path, but thirteen-year-olds might consider it a great place for mountain-biking or to catch an adrenaline rush. The truth is that biking these trails is forbidden, but that's what makes it exciting. That's why most afternoons, I bounded off the bus, chucked my backpack in the corner, and grabbed the telephone to call up my best friend, Chucky D. The plan was the same everyday: meet me on Talbot Road behind your house. And instantly, we were screaming down the hard-packed, dirt trail, me on my aqua-blue Specialized Hard-Rock and him on his Mongoose-full-suspension bike, feeling the wind whipping around us, yanking all the worries from school away, and making us feel immortal.

Every kid loves getting outside, but for me it represented a way to leave all of my troubles behind. Inside, especially at school, felt as if the rooms, the desks, the pencils themselves were sucking the strength out of me. It turns out that's exactly what was happening. When I was ten-years-old, I started to feel different than the other kids at school. Playing tag outside started to feel like a workout and the extra stress on my ankles and legs like a race. That fall I learned my fatigue had a name: CMT or Charcot Marie Tooth, a hereditary muscle weakness. Overtime, I have learned that exercise is of the utmost importance in order to lessen the effects of CMT. Activities like mountain biking and snowboarding not only provide exercise, but also combine my love for the outdoors.

Outside is a place where I feel strong and independent, energized by the fresh air around me, free from the everyday challenges that come with having this disease.

Today I have discovered how to be successful on my own, but getting here was very difficult and required the help of the right people. But first there were the wrong ones. Hand-writing, due to my CMT, has always been a struggle for me, and Mrs. Marx, my fifth-grade teacher, liked to show the class my half-completed assignments before ripping them up and throwing them in the garbage. Those were the days when I dreamed about the scene in *Ferris Bueller's Day Off* when he and Cameron Fry saved his girlfriend from school. How I wished a cherry-red-Ferrari-California was waiting outside for me. Even some teachers with good intentions unknowingly made work harder for me by not understanding the importance of having alternative ways to complete my work. Fortunately, there were people like Ms. Robie, my fifth-grade principal, who gave me a small laptop computer and told me to start typing my work. Her gift was a game changer, and I gained strategies that made school easier. Since then, I've added more tools to not only help with completing my work, but also with making me a stronger student. Ultimately, having a life-altering disability has not only made being independent a struggle, it also made gaining independence its own reward.

At 5,800-feet altitude, Heather Canyon is five times the elevation of Council Crest. It sits above the timberline, on the south side of Mt. Hood. This time I was not there with Chucky D, but a group of my friends from high school. Looking down at the valley stretched out beneath me, I realized how far I'd come. And with that, I jumped and turned my board down the hill, the flexible bamboo-base floated on top of the fresh powder. I went for a heel side turn and sprayed the powdered-sugar-snow straight up in my face. When I arrived where my friends waited, I slid in on my toe-side edge, covering them all with a thin layer of frost.

Ellie

Ellie's academic interests paint a gorgeous picture of how one can pursue various passions inside an undergraduate education. She's majoring in chemistry and studio art at Oregon State University, where she plans to pursue pharmacology research post-graduation. Ellie also serves as an inspiration to fellow students, after transferring colleges during her sophomore year to pursue greater research opportunities. Change is a theme she's noticed in her undergraduate journey and wants to encourage new college students that changing majors along the way is more common than you'd think, something that at first surprised her. Ellie's beautiful essay explores the paradoxical experience of growing up despite feeling a part of you is forever missing. Her essay is a powerful example of choosing a story that only she could tell.

WITH AND WITHOUT YOU

When Merav, my twin sister, was feeling healthy, I knew I was going to have a good day. On these days, Merav would support herself on the kitchen island, opening all the cabinets as she went along in the circle. The pattern was always the same. She opened seven cabinets with a creak, and I followed her, closing them with a thud. We would repeat this for hours. It always put a smile on her face, which put a smile on my face too.

Merav was born with a rare, spontaneous genetic disorder in which her brain was too small. She had trouble processing and sending information to her body because her brain did not fully develop. Due to this anomaly, parts of her brain would shut off causing her to have atonic, clonic, and grand mal seizures. As a child, my most vivid memories include Merav's seizures: the way she would stare off into space, as if she wasn't even there; the way her arms and legs would fall asleep; and the way her whole body would twitch. When Merav died at five-years-old, due to her heart stopping, I wondered what the world would be like without her.

While it's tempting to think that when Merav died she left me behind, I prefer to think she instead enhanced my capacity for empathy and kindness. I've often wondered about the scientific explanation for these qualities, and basic research on the neurology of twins reveals that we are predisposed to being social because of interactions in the womb. In other words, after Merav's death I didn't stop being a twin. Today I use my "twinness" to help the important people in my life: tutoring my friends in math and science, comforting my younger and homesick cousin who moved from Indonesia to the United States, and volunteering at a therapeutic barn for kids with special needs. This genuine compassion for the wellbeing of others is an important lens that I use to see the world.

Because of my experience with Merav, I am also driven to discover the unknown. Merav never had a diagnosis; her condition was a mystery. Today, my family still has hundreds of medical documents: karyotypes, MRIs, CT scans, blood tests, and more. Merav's life and the irresolvable nature of her illness inspire me to research medicine. In fact, just this year, I received an internship with Oregon Health & Science University in the Nephrology department, enabling me to assist in research on the genetics behind kidney disease and blood pressure. In this short time, I've discovered a fascination for this tiny yet significant organ: the thousands of genes that work together to make the kidneys function and how the removal of one gene can result in what nephrologists call "kidney injury." While the genetics involved in nephrology are not related to Merav, the field of genetics fascinates me because there is so much yet to be discovered.

Everyone knows that there are two kidneys in the human body, but they might forget that the body can function with only one kidney. This phenomenon occurs when a healthy kidney adapts to do the work of two. When Merav died, I had to adapt; I had gone through the most impressionable years of my life with a partner, but I had to finish the work of growing up on my own. The characteristics of empathy, kindness, and curiosity are all ways that I adapted and grew up to this changed world. These qualities have already served me well and will continue to shape me as I pursue what I love most: science and helping others.

Landry

Landry believes college will challenge you, but if you can master the art of "studying out loud" you'll do fine. The nursing major at Texas Christian University in Fort Worth says the ability to study with friends, or in the very least, repeat your notes out loud to yourself, is the secret to her college success thus far. Landry received admission into nursing programs at Baylor University and the University of Portland, but chose to attend Texas

Christian, where she was given the Faculty Scholarship, an annual $18,000 award. Upon graduation, Landry plans to work as an RN in pediatric oncology. Like Matthew's "Grocery Lessons," Landry chose an artifact—the teeter-totter—to help her organize her essay and arrive at surprising insights. Her essay reminds us how creativity doubles as critical thinking, by finding meaning in everyday experiences.

UPS & DOWNS:
THE VIEW FROM THE TEETER-TOTTER

When I was a kid, the teeter-totter was easily my favorite playground toy. I found a thrill from the feeling of my stomach dropping, my hair blowing up and down, and the hesitant, nervous trusting of the person across from you. You'd go up, and you could see the entire world; you'd go down, and you were below everyone, waiting anxiously to reach the top again. At recess, from kindergarten to fifth grade, the teeter-totter was my go-to; I can hardly remember ever doing anything else. What I didn't understand as a child was that the teeter-totter would be a metaphor for finding balance in life. Sometimes you're up, and you can see the whole world. Sometimes you're down, waiting anxiously to reach the top again. Sometimes, if you're lucky, you'll find the perfect weight to balance you in a joyful suspension in the very middle.

Up. My childhood was easy, and I came from a happy family with amazing parents and kind sisters. We took family vacations, went out to dinner, had game nights, and spent nearly all of our time with each other happily. This was like the feeling of being at the top of my teeter-totter; I didn't have to worry about anything except for the elation I felt. My parents took care of everything I needed, and I felt unburdened. This way of life went on for the majority of my childhood, until I realized how stressful the world could be.

Down. In my freshman year of high school, I took a service trip to Helene, Honduras. This was the first time my eyes had been opened to the injustices of the world and how unfair my life had been compared to many others. After this trip, my awareness of the world took a 180-degree turn. I began to volunteer for the marginalized members of my community-- the homeless in downtown Portland, adults with intellectual disabilities, and youth at my church. As a child, my idea of "down" was being upset over a cookie I didn't get, or falling on the sidewalk. I never could have imagined that experiencing the lows of others would produce such insight. This awareness taught me that there will always be disadvantaged people in the world, but it's up to me to choose how I want to participate in that world.

Balance. Most days I wouldn't describe my life as a senior at a college-prep high school as balanced. But occasionally, I get a moment of calm suspension in which my hectic, chaotic life delays itself. On Sundays, my family often has an unofficial, unplanned movie day. One of us will turn on a movie, and the rest of us will slowly join, after completing homework or coming home from church. The mutual silence and calm of my entire family together gives me a sense of peace, one where I feel inner balance, my inner teeter-totter so to speak.

I haven't been on a teeter-totter since I was eight years old. Only recently did I think about this, while watching the children I nanny play on a teeter-totter. They were completely carefree, unaware of the world's problems, of homelessness or starvation. Up. For a moment, I wanted to be them again, young and naive to the world. Down. I realized that knowledge about the world's problems creates opportunities to improve the world. Balanced. The feeling created when the world slows down and I spend time with people that lift me up.

Lauren

Lauren received admission into the University of San Francisco, Pacific University, Seattle Pacific, and Gonzaga, where she earned awards between $40,000 and $60,000 over four years. She ultimately chose to study human physiology at Gonzaga University, in Spokane, Washington, where she was awarded the Dussault Merit Scholarship and Gonzaga Grant, valued at $50,000 for her undergraduate education. Her generous scholarship to Gonzaga lifts a financial burden as she plans to attend graduate school to earn a degree in physical therapy, with dreams of working in sports medicine. Lauren's passion for health and fitness extends to her advice for new college students. "The 'freshman 15' is not a real thing," she reports, but highlights the importance of a healthy and active freshman lifestyle. Lauren says there's no real secret to avoiding weight gain, just the simple wisdom of managing your time and taking care of yourself. Lauren's essay examines how growing up as an only child shaped her world view and presents another great version of the Common Application's backstory prompt.

ON BEING AN ONLY

The average price of a bear from Build-a-Bear is $25, but add in the cost of clothes and shoes and it becomes a very expensive toy. But that didn't matter to me when I was six-years-old. I was shopping for my new best friend with a short list of criteria: it had to be pink; it had to be plush; and it had to be a girl. Looking back, I know exactly what I was up to; I was creating the sister I had always wanted. While some kids were leaving the store with their toys and best friends, I was leaving with something much more.

I have been an only child for my entire life. My parents got divorced when I was three-years-old, and I moved to Portland when I was seven. I left many friends behind, and I felt a new sense of loneliness with the move, as I met an unknown group of people who didn't know anything about me. I believed that if I had a sibling I wouldn't be alone, and my life would be easier. Seventeen years later, I still don't have any siblings, but I do have the unique perspective of an only child.

Today I am an innovative thinker and problem solver, and I learned these lessons by being an only. When I was younger and alone, I was my own best friend. I had to make up games for myself. Without a sibling, I would play house, making my toys take on roles that were left empty in my life. I, of course, would always play the mom. Playing house presented me with a problem: I was alone. If I was going to solve it, I needed to think creatively. When I was older, I used this trait to become a peer mediator in middle school; when peers had their own problems, I offered out-of-the-box solutions to their sometimes limited perspectives.

Some people think that being an only child means getting everything you want or every toy you ask for. But getting my Build-a-Bear was a special occasion. In fact, when I turned sixteen, my mom did not provide me with my own car, but instead handed me a short list of rules on how to use the family car instead. My mom's list included washing the car every two weeks and paying for my own gas. Her decision showed me that she recognized that I was trustworthy and responsible enough to drive the car, but that I wasn't independent just yet and still part of the family. I also learned that really important things, like cars, need to be earned; they aren't going to be given to me.

Sometimes I wonder what it would be like to have a sibling. To be perfectly honest and a little selfish, I wish my parents would have stayed together for one more year just so I could have a brother or sister. However, I have come to understand that there are people in my life that can fill the empty role of a sibling. In fact, last year when I attended my high school's Junior Encounter, I experienced a closeness with the other girls. The format of the encounter included receiving "palancas" or letters from our closest family and friends. The letters brought out many overwhelming emotions, forcing everyone to display our true selves to each other. I imagined that this experience was like living with other teenagers in a family where we would see and know everything about each other, something that my Build-a-Bear best friend could never do. When I was a child, all I wanted was something to keep me from feeling lonely. Today, however, I understand that security comes from the lessons I learned growing up as an only child, lessons about working hard, solving problems, and finding family in some of my closest friends.

Ava

As a high school soccer player, Ava was familiar with challenging practices and game-day competition. She uses her topic, her amazing adoption story from Kazakhstan, which revolves around one of the earliest photos of herself and her mom, to show the connection with her past and personality today. This bright and thoughtful student is a biology and premedical student at the University of Portland.

PICTURE OF ME

In the camera roll on my phone, I have a picture of a picture. I'm sitting on my young and beautiful mother's lap wearing a simple red sweater, with my wavy hair tied up in a delicate pink bow. My brother grips a yellow and turquoise basket in the background. At first glance, it appears my mother and I are both looking at the camera, but if you zoom in closely my dark brown eyes are looking at something else. Looking away may seem like an unimportant detail, but, for me, it reminds me of my story, the story of my mom flying 5,944 miles away from Oregon to meet me.

My mother flew to Kazakhstan as a single parent hoping to adopt my brother and me. After a whole year of my mom looking at websites, examining pictures, writing letters, filling out paper work, talking to friends and family, and many sleepless nights, she arrived at Children's Home #1, intent on adopting my brother and me. Typically, at the orphanage it was common to run up to the visitors, and the day my mom arrived, my brother did this with no problem. I, on the other hand, stood back. Embarrassed, the caregivers suggested another girl, but my mom refused. She adopted both me and my brother, and together we flew back home to Portland, where she raised us on her own, giving us the love and consistency we never had.

Unlike my brother, I was shy and observant, and I'm still a bit like this today. At the orphanage, I lived with many children but not many caretakers. This created a sense of independence but also questions about where I came from and who I belonged to. When I got older, my mom told us that when she brought us home we were very protective and careful with our toys, something she had observed from the orphanage. In Kazakhstan, we all had to share our belongings. Today, I wonder if being protective of my toys represented my need for answers. I couldn't control my surroundings, but I could control, even protect, the toys that belonged to me. Thankfully, sharing is not a problem anymore. In fact, most of my friends would describe me as a giving person.

Sometimes being quiet and observant can be challenging, but it's also served me quite well in other areas. As my soccer career has developed, I've excelled at positions that require the ability to see the whole field in order to direct other players. Specifically, when playing forward I have to be ready and watchful for "offsides," a penalty called when an offensive player is ahead of a defensive player. If I get called for offsides, our team not only loses possession but also momentum. On the other hand, the best way to score is to watch and wait for a defensive error and be ready to take advantage of the mistake.

Thinking back on my picture, my two-year-old self had no idea what was happening. I didn't know that I'd have a mother that would give up everything just for me and love me unconditionally. I didn't know that my life was about to change forever. I'm so thankful for my brave mom who traveled over 5,000 miles to choose a shy, little girl like me.

Anika

With a love of improv comedy, Anika is active in the theatre arts community at Portland State University, located in the heart of beautiful Portland, Oregon. As a communications major, PSU awarded Anika a $5,000 merit scholarship to attend. She's the social media coordinator for the Jewish Student Union and an Alpha Chi Omega collegiate member. Like many college students, Anika boasts her cooking skills revolve around making a "fairly good bowl of noodles." She plans to pursue a career in the arts after graduation. Anika's bittersweet and humorous essay shows us how to balance a serious topic with lightness and personality in order to emerge as a real person. Her method for organizing her experiences into unique lessons provides a model for how to fit your life story into 650 words or less.

WOLFIE THE WOLF & ME

Wolfie the wolf was the closest thing I had to a human baby as a child. I remember holding her, singing her lullabies, and tucking her in at night. Occasionally, I would stuff her under my shirt, yank her out, and gloriously perform birth. When I was nine my aunt got pregnant, and I was overjoyed. I wanted to hear the whole process. I even went to the baby shower, willingly. *What nine-year- old does that?* The answer is a girl who is excited-- excited to be pregnant--and have her own children. Becoming a mother has always been my dream, but for now, let me tell you about my current fork in the road.

1. Plan but don't over plan. Be open.

Today I am a flexible person, but when I was younger I had a plan. When I was thirteen, I had a pain in my side. After many doctor visits, too many blood tests, and one CT scan, I discovered I had MRKH. MRKH, also known as Mayer-Rokitansky-Kuster-Hauser syndrome, meant that when I was in-vitro my uterus didn't fully form. This news meant I would never carry my own children. I felt like a fraud. Instead of fitting in with other girls my age, I felt like there were bright, flashing arrows pointing toward my nonexistent womb.

2. You can't eat chocolate every day; don't eat your feelings.

I have an inner strength today that I knew nothing about when I was 13. When I was a small child, I decided to attend the only all girls high school in Oregon. It never occurred to me this was a bad idea until later, but being surrounded by girls throughout the week meant I couldn't escape my biggest fear. Here I was at age fourteen trying to understand if I was a girl or not, and yet I was surrounded constantly by estrogen. All I did that freshman year, along with my friends, was eat, complain, sleep, and repeat this cycle. I gained weight and fast. I decided to make some changes. I started running and lifting weights; I discovered kale, bell peppers, spinach, and roasted yams, and I switched schools. These changes started to feel like Christmas every day. Maybe not every day, but I did learn to honor my sadness and get off the couch.

3. Everything's going to be okay, but it will take awhile.

One of the most important lessons I have learned before leaving for college is that we are all in it together. However, you can only be a full member of the community if you accept yourself. I discovered this truth by attending the young women's conference for MRKH in Boston, two years after my diagnosis. We sat down scared, nervous, and full of danishes. My internal battle included: the female species (*would they like me?*), but it also covered bigger battlefields like how I still didn't accept my anatomy; this conference challenged me to see myself as I really am. I sat down next to a mother and daughter duo, their smiles welcomed me, telling me everything was okay. The flashing arrows turned off.

I thought the best part about playing with Wolfie was she was my baby, but now I know the best part was that I was happy. My journey has taught me to be strong, helped me rediscover my confidence, and provided me with lifelong friends. Some people might say I am unlucky because of my difference, but I say I am lucky because I can tackle problems, honor sadness, and overall be filled with strength I never knew I had. I have learned a life lesson: plans don't always work out. I know I will pick up a child some day and hopefully fall in love. But until then I will take the lessons given me by my life's unexpected twist and keep learning.

Oliver

Oliver received admission into Gonzaga University's School of Engineering and Applied Sciences to study civil engineering. He was awarded the school's Regent Scholarship, an $18,500 scholarship renewable annually. As he looks into the future, he foresees using his engineering skills to work in Central and South America to help improve infrastructure in developing countries and in his words, "make a difference in the world." As you read his essay, you'll discover Oliver's family value of travel and exploration, but even Oliver was surprised to learn that 52 percent of Gonzaga's undergraduates will apply for study abroad, a statistic he found encouraging as it matches his own plans to study next year in Madrid, Spain. His common application essay explores how he learned the meaning of culture firsthand, as an elementary school student traveling the world with his family for one year. Oliver's essay shows us how to use our experiences to invite readers into an insightful and philosophical conversation about family values.

FINDING YOUR PLACE ON THE MAP

When my parents announced they had a plan for us to travel around the world for ten months, I didn't know how to feel. As a second grader, I had just begun to form friendships with my classmates, and I felt anxious about leaving my comfort zone. What if I didn't like any of the food in Germany? What was life really like in Morocco? How would Santa bring us presents in

Vietnam? Packing my large backpack on our last day in the States, I sat down and started flipping through the glossy pages of a travel guide. Glancing upwards, I noticed the collection of multicolored pins sticking out of a large map of the world, marking our destinations of the journey ahead. Reading the names of each strange city, I asked my mom, "What *is* culture?" She laid down our passports and patiently replied, "Culture is what makes every place different." At the time, I didn't really understand the true meaning of my Mom's insightful words, which I quickly forgot, focusing my attention instead on ensuring my favorite toys were packed safely.

My family has always valued experiences over things, citing that memories last forever and stuff doesn't. Now as a seventeen-year-old I can see how very true that statement is. Over the following ten-month journey, we circled the globe, hopping from pin to pin, visiting exactly eighteen countries. When we returned home, we realized the expedition had left us with an incredible desire for more cultural experiences, and three years later we moved to London for two and a half years. Eventually, we made our way back to Portland, but the trips didn't stop, and every summer meant another vacation to an unfamiliar country.

Our trip around the world started in Tokyo, Japan's capital city. Previously, Japan had only represented a distant island country my dad had marked with a yellow pin on our map, but I will always remember what I learned there. Stepping off the plane after a thirteen-hour flight, my uncle, one of my many language and travel role models, greeted us in Japanese. "Kon'nichiwa," I repeated, trying to match his smooth accent as we walked through the streets of urban Tokyo. Listening to the fast-talking Japanese people and seeing their strange characters written on every street sign, I thought I had discovered the foundation of culture itself: language. However, when I sat with my legs crossed on the kitchen floor, eating beef curry with rice for breakfast while learning silly Japanese phrases, I realized culture had to be a combination of a distinct language and food. But soon I discovered more aspects of culture, and with each subtle alteration, I learned that culture was a complex idea I had yet to understand.

The idea of culture continued to puzzle me throughout my childhood, and it wasn't until our move to London that I began to develop a working definition for myself. Classmates born in Singapore with Pakistani roots, teachers from Germany and the flurry of languages spoken on public transport created a melting pot of ideas and identities. It was London's strange combination of backgrounds that helped me to understand that culture isn't simply a mix of a unique language and type of food but a way of life that represents who you are in the world. My time in London gave me the ability to connect and understand other people's personal stories with a new perspective on life.

My family has always encouraged me to be independent and now that my life is changing course, the move to college means adding places to my own map. Traveling the world at a young age and moving to a foreign country wasn't easy, however, the many cultural experiences I encountered during my travels with my family have changed who I am and how I see the world.

Ben

Ben received acceptance into all five of his schools, with generous financial offers from institutions ranging from the University of Puget Sound, Oregon State University, and Pacific University. Linfield College offered him the most impressive award with a $24,500 scholarship and a $5,000 diversity grant, renewable all four years. As an award-winning varsity pitcher at a 6A high school, Ben says one of his hardest decisions came from whether or not to pursue baseball in college. Ultimately, Ben narrowed his search to the Northwest and chose the Honors College at Oregon State University, where he plans to study biology on a pre-medicine track and play intramural baseball. In his essay, Ben examines cultural identity in a humorous and insightful piece that reminds readers how little children often see the world, overlooking racial differences in favor of physical strengths. As he notes in his essay, today Ben is proud of his Asian heritage and celebrated the holidays this year, per usual, in Hawaii with his family.

UNDERCOVER IDENTITY

"Brrring!" Sometimes when I think back to middle school, it all seems like one long succession of bells: bells to signal the start of school, bells to tell you you're late, and bells to open your eyes to the realities of growing up. On my second day of 6th grade, as the lunch bell rang out across the school, I shuffled out of my English class and stepped into a crowded, unfamiliar hallway. I stood there for a moment and took in the spectacle in front of me. To my left lockers were slamming, on my right there were people shouting, and straight ahead a familiar boy walked toward me with a big grin. Even now it's amazing that I heard him above the chaos, but his words rang out loud and clear: "Yoooooo what's up my Asian?!" I wasn't sure what he meant. I gave a half smile and played along with the comment. On the long walk to the cafeteria, I concentrated on my shoelaces and pondered what he'd said. When the final bell rang that day, I went home with one realization: I am different.

It wasn't really a secret that I was Asian, but it had never really occurred to me before. I knew my mom grew up in Hawaii and that her parents were from Japan. My middle name is Makoto for goodness sake. It just hadn't been brought to my attention until I reached middle school. Ironically, the kid who high-fived me that day was also technically Asian, but it's not like we talked about it. In elementary school, we measured differences by who was tallest, fastest, or funniest, not racial distinctions. It wasn't that I thought being Asian was bad; I just didn't think any label truly summarized me. For the next few years, I struggled with the contrast of what people said I was and how I actually felt. Looking back, if I were able to give my 6th-grade-self advice, I would tell him not to be so serious and to realize that everyone is different in their own way. I would tell him that learning to accept yourself will allow you to be your own individual who is both unique and likeable.

Learning to laugh at yourself is probably the best advice I could give anyone starting middle school. Being able to openly acknowledge your own differences means that no one can hold them over you. This skill translates to other aspects of my life. For example, as a starting pitcher for my high school team heckling is not uncommon. You can either take people's comments internally and believe their insults, or you can laugh it off and strike out the next batter. Besides, first team all-league is a title that speaks for itself.

I suppose you could argue that laughing at yourself doesn't actually solve the problem, that it's just a way of deflecting people's attention…and you'd be right. It's more like one half of the solution. The other half comes with the actual acceptance of who you are as a person. On a recent trip to Hawaii, we celebrated the new year with our usual tradition of lighting off fireworks and having Mochi soup in the morning. As I took a bite of the salted Buri fish and the slimy mochi, it occurred to me that I really enjoy doing this each year. The soup is a part of my heritage that I can be proud of, and led me to realize that being Asian is not only okay, but good: even though it doesn't actually taste that great.

Asher

Asher had been dreaming of attending St. Mary's College of California, in the Bay Area, since his sophomore year of high school. He credits his diligence in completing his college applications with his opportunity to not only attend his first-choice school but also to receive a scholarship that totals a third of his tuition from the St. Mary's Leclercq and Endowment Scholarships. For Asher, St. Mary's has offered him the rolling and scenic hills of California, away from the bustle of a big city, yet still close enough to visit favorite places like Santa Cruz, San Francisco, Oakland, and Lake

Tahoe. The magic of the college's setting creates the backdrop for his study in business, already with varied work experiences while in college. From falls spent bussing tables to summers as a full-time nanny, Asher wants to give future college students some surprising wisdom he learned along the way: you won't receive internships from the classroom. In fact, Asher says, "I've received LinkedIn profiles at bars, business cards while waiting tables, and offers from the parents of kids I've nannied." He believes the college experience gives you back whatever you invest and plans on making good on these internship offers before he graduates. Asher's beautiful essay that details the lovely Paulina Lake in Central Oregon shows us how to use a place to tell a story about ourselves.

HOME AWAY FROM HOME

Gray clouds move in, replacing sunshine with darkness. Thunder bounces off the thousand-foot volcanic walls, echoing back into our campground. A bolt of lightning strikes the middle of the lake, lighting it up out of the darkness. The rain falls steady, never letting up. Back home people sit in their houses, protected from the storm. Out here we have nowhere to go. Yet I feel strangely safe. Standing in the rain, watching as the thunderous clouds move in and out giving back what little sun we got. Even in the biggest storms, I am calm. Something about the simplicity of standing there, observing nature in such a violent form. Your focus is on one thing, the storm and nothing else.

The unpredictability of Paulina Lake is what makes me feel so at home there. Although I split time between my mom and dad, I've moved six times in the last fourteen years of my life. Every week I pack the majority of what I own into a few suitcases and move to my other family. Change feels natural to me. Even though my family has camped at Paulina for the last seven years, each year brings new challenges. We never know what kind of weather we'll get. This forces us to adapt quickly, just like how I adapt to changes in my life at home.

Being able to adapt to change allows me to be more resourceful. Camping at Paulina brings out this quality. The first night we camped on Paulina the wind reached gusts over 45 miles per hour. We tried multiple times, but couldn't light our campfire with the heavy wind. We had a huge tarp that we used as a wall. We tied it to a few trees, creating a shield from the wind coming off the lake. At home, there would never be a need to engineer something like this. If it's windy, you go inside. Here at Paulina, there is no escaping the storm. The wind would have torn our tents, the only thing that sheltered us from the relentless rainstorms. By thinking on our feet and using what we had, we saved ourselves from a vacation-ending disaster.

There is a natural relationship between resourcefulness and gratitude. When we camp, we don't get the luxuries like dishwashers or big beds. We have to carry our water, hand-clean our dishes. We don't have heaters or air conditioning. For a week, we take a break from our complicated lives to live a little simpler. When I return home after a long week of camping, I'm so grateful for the first night's sleep in my bed, for the shower with actual hot water and especially for the electricity that powers all of our appliances and gadgets. Although we miss all this camping, it is also one of the reasons why camping is so enjoyable. Without electricity, everything is simple; being unplugged from the Internet, phone and other communication gives us a break for the time we spend at Paulina.

As I get ready to graduate high school and move on to college, I'm reminded of the storms at Paulina. The changes in my life will be substantial: moving out, living in a new city, being on my own, making new friends. Just like the storm, I will encounter unforeseen issues and complications. College may occasionally ask me to create a new wall of tarps; luckily all these years of camping at Paulina have refined my capabilities.

PART III:
HEROIC TALES FROM COLLEGE-BOUND SENIORS

"What really knocks me out is a book that,
when you're all done reading it, you wish the author
that wrote it was a terrific friend of yours and you could
call him up on the phone whenever you felt like it."
—Holden Caulfield from J.D. Salinger's *The Catcher in The Rye*

14

COMING-OF-AGE STORIES

Magena

After receiving admissions into Cornell University, the University of Michigan, and UCSD, Magena ultimately chose to study bioengineering at the University of Washington. She is a distinguished National Merit Scholar winner and studies in the honors program at UW. Additionally, she is the recipient of the Bausch + Lomb Honorary Science Award and the University of Washington Honors Program Scholarship. In just her first three years of college, Magena conducted research in a cellular biomechanics lab, resulting in an exclusive invitation from Emerging Researchers National, who flew her to Washington, DC to present her work at their conference. Before she left home for Seattle's U-District, Magena could be seen running miles and miles throughout her local neighborhood, pursing her other passion: running. Her refreshing essay highlights how simple experiences not only create profound effects in our lives but also make tremendous essay topics. Her insightful retrospective on getting a haircut spotlights the power of playing the role of the protagonist in your own life.

NEW DO: NEW YOU

I have been mistaken for a boy more times than I can count. I'm not abnormally tall, nor am I excessively muscled, nor do I wear jeans that sag below my boxers. I don't even ride a skateboard. What is it, then, that causes people to take one glance at me and think, "boy"?

Well, I have short hair.

For years I had worn my hair in deliberate imitation of every other teenage girl. My hairstyle was not an expression of myself; on the contrary, the long hair carefully arranged into ponytails, or hanging loose and flowing like a Garnier Nutrisse commercial, was a way to mask my individuality. I was embarrassed by everything that made me different – my quirks, my sense of humor – and so I set about masking my individuality behind a generic face. My hair was the perfect tool to create this mask because it was the one thing I could absolutely control.

Nothing extraordinary happened to change me. I continued unaltered in my philosophy through middle school and high school, yet to my surprise I took a few risks: joining the cross-country team, leading a Battle of the Books club to victory at State, and competing in Oregon's Science Olympiad. I discovered that my unique qualities were perhaps things to be proud of, not hidden. I began to feel confident, and I found I could be anyone I wanted. I felt liberated. I felt like a rebel. I felt strangely dangerous. I wanted to do something really wild, something to proclaim my newfound boldness. I decided to cut off my hair.

My new haircut was *short*, and I wasn't sure I liked it. In fact, I was sure that people would judge me harshly for rejecting the idea that femininity requires long hair. *Will people laugh when I walk into school? Will they notice my right ear is higher than my left? Is this how Hester Prynne felt wearing the scarlet letter for adultery?* So, when people's responses were overwhelmingly positive, it was totally unexpected. Even a girl I hadn't spoken to in years told me I had inspired her by rejecting conformity in order to express my individuality. I hadn't known that a personal risk like cutting my hair could have such widespread approval, and I found I wasn't the only one asking what "being yourself" means.

The process of growing up is remarkably glacial: every day nothing happens, but after years of nothing happening you suddenly find that a fundamental shift has occurred whether you knew it or not. My shift was the gradual wearing away of the mask that I once needed so badly. I found that, by cutting my hair, I had wiped clean all preconceived notions of my character. I was struck by a heady sense of *possibility*, the idea that I could defy even my own idea of who I was. Who knows what I'll do next. Maybe it's time to get that skateboard.

Sarah G.

Sarah tells aspiring undergrads a sobering truth: the college years just may be too short—that is, if you want to dedicate yourself to academics and fun. Still, this Princeton University student, accepted through early decision, is doing her best while pursuing her degree in Middle Eastern studies. Sarah's impressive resume includes awards for National Merit Scholar finalist, the National Peace Award, and scholarships from notable companies like Nordstrom and Radio Disney. Prior to college, Sarah spent her summers teaching in Cambodia and has since interned for the United Nations and Senator Jeff Merkley. In 2018, Sarah became one of Princeton University's Streicker Fellows for International Studies, receiving an award to pursue a research project in Amman, Jordan. She plans to work in national security and counterterrorism after graduation and eventually pursue a graduate degree in her field. Sarah knew when she applied early decision to Princeton the competition would be fierce, so she chose to stand out by letting her accomplishments from her academic resume speak for themselves and instead use her essay to showcase quirk, not to mention her initiative, ingenuity, and grit. Her remarkable essay on creating historical YouTube videos begins with a dramatized scene, as she plunders her mother's wardrobe.

DATE WITH CHARLEMAGNE

I was raiding my mom's closet, and I knew exactly what I was looking for. Crawling into the darkness of her wardrobe, I found the floor--length, black gown. I emerged to plunder her jewelry box and extract a pair of dangerously long, rhinestone earrings. To complete the ensemble, I descended to the basement and unlatched my old costume chest. There it was: the princess tiara from Halloweens past. I quickly placed it on my head and raced back to the living room. It was time for my date with Charlemagne.

When I first met Charlemagne, I knew he needed my help. I was thirteen, and he was 1,269, but it wasn't his age that was the problem. What I couldn't understand was why his legendary exploits failed to inspire the same fascination in my middle school peers as they did in me. The guy discarded more wives and mistresses than a Hollywood leading man and had more kids than the Duggar family on TLC. He could have dominated today's tabloids, yet the dust of time covered Charlemagne like a shroud.

Before middle school, reading books had satisfied my fascination with history. But learning about the first Holy Roman Emperor inspired me to bring history to life. Any modern PR maven would consider Charlemagne a lost--cause client, but I took him on with relish. Maybe my friends weren't interested in him on paper, but what if I brought him to life through something to which all teenagers could relate…popular music?

And so, I decided to fix history's public image problem. I transformed the lyrics of popular songs into lessons that resurrected historical figures and eras. With the help of Garage Band, I recorded myself singing the new versions. I donned costumes like my mother's black dress and used a camcorder to direct myself as onscreen talent. A bit of editing with iMovie, and my finished music videos were uploaded to YouTube. "Charlemagne," a rendition of Lady Gaga's "Telephone," was soon followed by "Inca-licious" set to "Fergalicious"; "California Gold" set to "California Gurls"; and "Galileo" set to "Dynamite" by Taio Cruz. Sometimes I searched for the right songs. Sometimes they found me. When a serendipitous alignment between modern rhythms and encyclopedic facts occurred, things just clicked.

My friends and teachers loved it. People around the world loved it. I was surprised by how much I loved it. Sharing my work and passion felt great. There was nothing better than hearing classmates singing my lyrics as they walked through the halls at school or reading the messages that poured into my inbox from thousands of followers as far-flung as Japan, Germany, and Brazil. Teachers throughout the country incorporated my videos into their history curriculums, and even TED Talks referenced my endeavors.

As educators repurposed my videos, I began to discover my own purpose. Sure, I was good at making videos, but I uncovered other passions too. In starting a chapter of the United Nations Foundation's Girl Up campaign at my high school, I became a PR agent for a segment of society even more disregarded than the subject of history: adolescent girls in low-income countries. I was named a Teen Advisor and International Co-Chair of the organization, and even spoke at the United Nations about my advocacy for teenage girls -- girls who are as ambitious as Charlemagne, as brave as Joan of Arc, and as clever as Cleopatra. Girls who deserve to make their own history.

My YouTube videos are now a thing of my past, as I have shifted my focus from the intrigues of the past to the challenges of the present. But I still reflect on these creations and sometimes jot down new lyrics. Occasionally I even try on that black dress. And just the other day, I turned on the radio and thought how much Ke$ha's "Tik Tok" sounded like "Plymouth Rock."

Kathryn

Kathryn is one of the lucky few who discovered a passion early and used the college application process to find programs suited to provide her with training for her future fascinating career. After acceptances into the engineering programs at Purdue, Baylor, UCSB, Oregon State University, and UCLA, Kathryn chose to study bioengineering at the Henry Samueli School of Engineering and Applied Science at UCLA, where she was awarded the Stanton and Stockwell Architects Scholarship and the Faculty Fund for Undergraduate Scholarships. In her three years at UCLA, Kathryn has pursued her studies alongside impressive positions such as a motion analysis assistant in the UCLA Orthopedic Surgery Department and director of outreach for the Girls Who Code chapter at UCLA, as well as participating in the UCLA Marathon Club. After graduation, she plans to work with athletes in motion analysis to help them improve their performance. Her hard-work ethic is matched by a sunny attitude, noting that despite what you hear about college food, UCLA's cuisine was her favorite part of freshman year. She proudly reminds everyone they are ranked number one for food in the nation, for the second year running according to Niche's "2018 Best College Food in America." Kathryn's essay explores a sobering turning point in her life as she and her family travel to Africa and meet the orphans in a small village. While many teachers and high school counselors urge students to steer clear of travel abroad or mission trips, Kathryn's essay shows us how to treat meaningful topics with an authentic touch, as she recounts the way little Gloria changed her life.

GLORIA

The cry of a baby haunts me to this day. I am unable to hear a cry without thinking of Gloria, about the time when I left her, never to return. I remember the image of one hand grasping the wooden bar of the make-shift crib, while the other reached outward stretching towards me, as if reaching for something on a shelf that was ten feet tall. I wish I never looked back to see her eyes, filling with tears, slowly being taken over by despair. However, that single glance over my shoulder, as I exited the door and left her, is what made a permanent mark on my life.

Before my trip to Kenya, my life felt like living under a warm and cozy blanket. I was the second generation to live in our family home, in a neighborhood where the sound of children playing on the green lawns was frequent and the sight of families walking on the clean sidewalks was common. My childhood followed a certain rhythm: mom picked me up from school daily, never even one minute late; crust-less sandwiches and apple perfectly sliced apples awaited me; and I did my homework at the kitchen table to the sounds of my mom preparing dinner. Even my acute asthma was handled with reassurance—the countless visits to the school nurse's office, multiple trips to the hospital for IVs and breathing treatments, and even a call to the fire department were swift and successful.

Unlike my life, Gloria lived exposed to the dangers of the world. At seven months old, she had already moved out of the cardboard home. Telephone wires surrounded her house, creating a maze just to get to the front door, and the sounds of screams were piercing and constant. Her mother died of electrocution, her father was blind and unable to care for her, and she was separated from her seven-year-old brother, as no orphanage would take both children. On top of this, she was malnourished, yet no one was concerned with her health, nor did her family have the money to give her the medical care that she needed.

My experience with Gloria led me to a bittersweet realization about life. For seven days, I carried Gloria everywhere I went, fed her bottles of fortified milk, bounced her on my knee as I sang her the "Trotty Trotty" nursery rhyme. I did not let her out of my sight. The night before I left Gloria's piercing screams and flooding tears began. The sounds pierced the ears of everyone around and awakened the other babies. Somehow, she knew. She knew I was leaving just like her mother, father, and brother had all done before me. Leaving Gloria was the hardest thing I had ever done because I knew that there was nothing I could do to help her—I was only fourteen-years-old. When I left Kenya, I took with me this unbearable knowledge: there will always be children suffering and no blanket to keep them safe and warm.

It has been four years since I last saw Gloria. Even though the experience left me with a deep sorrow, I have gained a valuable perspective on my life: I have a newfound gratitude for the life that I live, and I have realized the importance of serving others. Every month, I work at Goose Hollow Family Shelter, where I play with homeless children. Through this experience, I am able to fulfill my desire to help children like Gloria; sometimes I even daydream about the future and adopting a child. I keep a picture of Gloria above my desk to remind me of her gift: no matter the challenges that my life brings me, the struggles of homeless children around the world are beyond comparison to my loving and stable life.

Matthew

Matthew studies business marketing at his first-choice school, Chapman University, in Orange, California. He encourages applicants to work toward their dream school, as he received admission into Chapman, despite his lower test scores in comparison to their competitive average. He credits finishing his senior year with a great GPA, while playing two varsity sports, and working hard on his application essay with his eventual acceptance at Chapman. In keeping with his strong work ethic, Matthew is in pursuit of the ideal men's clothing internship, with plans to continue graduate studies after college. In addition to classes and career plans, he thinks undergrads will love college because, "Meeting new people never gets old." Like previous essays that examine unique turning points, Matthew chose a trip to the grocery store to show how growing up includes moments both big and small. The success of his essay depends on the well-placed lines that acknowledge the seeming absurdity of grocery-trip-as-coming-of-age story and yet the surprising truth that this day contained valuable lessons.

GROCERY LESSONS

As I turned the wheel, I felt the lip of the curb hit my tires as I parked in the farthest empty spot from the grocery store. I walked through the half empty spaces, rechecked my pockets, and studied my phone: "Fruits, coffee creamer, chicken." I stood at the entrance. And as a woman exited through the automatic doors, the cold air conditioning awakened me to another error: I'd forgotten a cart. I turned around. A few seconds later, I finally walked inside-- this time feeling prepared and a little more comfortable, since I had something to hold onto.

On a warm Saturday this September, I sat outside on my patio steps hoping to find anything to occupy my time. My mom walked outside to get the daily mail. She noticed something was wrong, and I simply responded that I was bored. As a stereotypical Italian mother, she began aiming meaningless ideas at me, while I kept brushing them off. Then the worst of all came. She suggested I go to the grocery store and quickly rattled off a list. Strangely, at seventeen years old, I had never been to the grocery store by myself. As the youngest of four children, going to the grocery store had only ever meant tagging along and staying close to the cart. Now as my role changed from a cute cart passenger to paying customer, the fear truly struck me. I looked at my list one more time and began.

Apples: My first stop was the produce aisle. I was determined to look like an expert. I tossed a few Fuji's into the air trying to remember my mother's instructions. A good apple is heavy or light? I chose the lighter one and ripped off a plastic bag, dropping them smoothly inside. I later learned that I should have picked the heavy apples. In the end, however, it didn't matter which apple I chose, rather it was that I was making choices. Participating, it turns out, is more fun than watching.

Coffee Creamer: My next stop was more complicated than my last. Not only is the dairy aisle in the back of the store but the aisles are the narrowest. I glanced at the list but noticed she did not specify which coffee creamer. Coffee-Mate or International Delight? Carton or plastic bottle? Hazelnut or Original? After blocking the passageway for five minutes, I realized many unhappy people were waiting. I hurriedly grabbed original. As I rolled my cart away, I noticed that the pressure to be polite caused me to make a quick decision. Luckily, it was only creamer. But as I thought about politeness, I realized it is not always the correct answer, especially when the stakes are higher.

Chicken: My final stop was the deli counter. Before I left the house, I received a short lecture to order thinly-sliced chicken, not turkey. My mother proceeded to tell me that the butcher would warn me that thinly sliced chicken falls apart. I shrugged it off then, yet when I politely asked the butcher for mom's precise requirements, he warned me that it does indeed fall apart. I ordered it anyway. I laughed when I realized my mom, once again, was right. But I also recognized the value in insisting on what I want. Unlike the dairy aisle, I hung with the discomfort as I advocated for myself.

I clicked the button, the garage door opened, and I parked the car. My mom waited with anticipation, but I confidently unloaded the groceries. After all, I had already lead my senior class's twelve-mile pilgrimage, powered through three brutal football seasons of daily doubles, and survived two weeks in Nicaragua. Nonetheless, the trip to the store felt like a small but significant personal achievement. I feel ready for whatever comes next. Still, I hope she doesn't ask me to get the Thanksgiving turkey.

Zanzan

Zanzan was accepted early decision to Johns Hopkins University, where she majors in molecular and cellular biology. She shadows at Johns Hopkins University Hospital and Oregon Health Sciences University and started her first year of college as a research intern at Dr. Xin Chen's lab at JHU. She serves on the marketing team for the JHU chapter of Junior MD, as well as the Women in Business marketing team. Zanzan plans to study neurology or oncology in medical or graduate school. She loves her time at JHU but has a tip for lonesome parents who want to see their college student more: get them a dog. Zanzan says she travels back home to Portland often to see Kona, her new puppy.

THE MORE QUESTIONS, THE BETTER

Fingers trembling, arms aching, and heart racing, I held the delicate flask inside of the sterilized hood. It was the first time I had been left alone in the easily contaminated cell culture room. I popped on my gloves, sprayed my hands and arms with 70% ethanol, and moved the cell flask under the microscope lens. Stringy, sticky glioblastoma appeared in the bright image produced. I imagined the cells strewn inside of a human brain--the best neurosurgeon in the world would not be able to remove every cell.

The first time I saw an image of cancer cells wasn't through a microscope, but through a computer screen. After learning about my best friend's mom's diagnosis of a noncancerous brain tumor, the Google searches began. Somehow, the tumor managed to become cancerous, and she passed away within a year of her initial diagnosis, raising questions in my mind. Last summer, I had a shot at acquiring some answers. Words alone couldn't answer my questions, but what was said to me and the people who spoke them have undoubtedly impacted my pursuit of knowledge.

"All students will be paired with a mentor; your mentor's lab is the lab in which you will work this summer." These simple instructions ignited my ambition right away; I knew I'd have to fight for one of the two coveted spots in the neuro-oncology lab at Oregon Health & Science University. I quickly typed up an email to Dr. Tammy Martin, who was in charge of mentor assignments through the Partnership for Scientific Inquiry Program. My lab acceptance taught me that my ambition put me in the right place, but the lab-work itself taught me something else.

"I like to think of the cancer cells I culture as a little garden," Dree, a research assistant, mused, as she was showing me the ropes of the cell culture room on my first day. When I started my cancer research, I wanted to be a part of the team that kills cancer cells forever. However, cell culture, a necessary part of research, is all about keeping the organisms alive and healthy. A neuro-oncology lab, a place where I was literally studying the brain, taught me how to expand my own mind to new ways of thinking.

"You can do everything, but you can't be the best at everything," my research mentor said to me as we ate lunch. My mentor, Cymon, is witty, bright, and determined--not to mention a fifth year M.D. PhD student who's probably the smartest person I've met. No one had ever said that to me before, and for the first time, someone I looked up to had encouraged my goals. Yet she wasn't just telling me to tackle everything, despite my own stubbornness to do so. Instead, she provided me with a choice, a challenge even, to fight hard for my dreams--but to choose my battles wisely.

My questions haven't been answered by these words, but my ambition has been inspired by the people who spoke them. Questions are the driving force behind my curiosity and love of science—the more questions, the better. In the future, I'll still have to fight for opportunities, continue to challenge my beliefs, and accept that I can't be the best at everything. I feel ready for that. I haven't been to the lab since August, but I still think about it all the time. Seeding cells independently always sent a rush of adrenaline through my veins, and I felt unstoppable. That's a feeling I want to experience again and again.

Brian

Like many students who apply early decision, Brian ultimately had to turn down his acceptances at other schools. In his case, this meant leaving a Presidential Scholarship at Gonzaga to attend his first-choice school, Trinity College in Hartford, Connecticut. However, Brian says this was an easy decision. After touring many exclusive STEM schools and other East Coast liberal arts colleges, he felt at home at Trinity the moment he stepped foot on campus. *Forbes* calls Trinity College a "Little Ivy," due to its prestigious reputation, along with its excellent 10:1 student to faculty ratio. Brian says he knew he wanted a college experience with a strong engineering program inside of a liberal arts education, as he plans to work in a field that utilizes computer science and engineering. Brian loves the outdoors, so it's no surprise his favorite sport is soccer—a sport played in the rain, sun, and occasionally snow and maybe even next year at Trinity. His essay looks at his experience of making the varsity soccer team as a freshman and emphasizes a mantra he learned from his dad, "Hard work pays off," illustrating Brian's family values and overall grit. Moreover, the lessons he learns from soccer translate to life on and off the field, wisdom he'll need as he continues a rigorous engineering education.

TURF LESSONS

Growing up, whenever I didn't finish my writing assignments, my dad would tell me: "Hard work ALWAYS pays off." On the days where I wanted to sleep instead of working out: "Hard work ALWAYS pays off." Even when I learned how to cook scrambled eggs: "Hard work ALWAYS pays off." I embraced this motto as I pushed through a particularly difficult soccer practice. I was dead last, and not by a small margin. I rounded the corner. I picked up the pace. My mind went blank. I focused on not falling over when I heard a yell: "23 minutes." The goal was to be done by 21. I was certain the other players were changing into their cleats already, when I heard my teammates cheering me on. I forced my legs to go faster, faster, faster, and sprinted the final stretch. I barely crossed the finish line when I collapsed onto the soft turf. As the rest of my new team took the field, every unfamiliar player walked by and gave me words of congratulations.

I was certainly the smallest on the varsity team, and I had to work for everything. Consider this: me, a 5-foot 7-inch, 135-pound freshman, squaring up against a 6-foot, 210-pound senior. Not only was this matchup a regular occurrence, but also a perfect metaphor for the barriers I had to overcome. The heightened expectations pushed me physically, and finding my place among the upperclassmen challenged me emotionally. Little did I know, I would need more than my dad's motto to make it.

The first thing I learned from squaring up against players three years older and 70-pounds heavier is this: if you think you're going to get crushed, you're going to get crushed. A lifetime of competitive soccer brought speed, skills, and a sense of the game that veteran players couldn't anticipate. It's hard to get crushed when you're sprinting around them. I've seen my experience with soccer translate directly into schoolwork. When my google calendar illuminates tomorrow's date with a test in first and second periods, a presentation in fifth, and a soccer game later, the uphill battle feels impossible. I remind myself what's possible and go one step at a time. With this inner motivation, I've learned to believe in myself. I still follow my dad's motto, with an added implication: capability comes from hard work, but self-belief is the hidden strength behind it.

The second lesson I learned is that commonalities are not necessary for friendship. I had zero friends on my new soccer team, but I knew I thrived from close bonds. Until then, my friends fit a specific description: shared my interests, shared my classes, shared my age. In other words, the best kind of friend was somebody just like me. Suddenly, I had to work harder to learn about my teammates' lives. Not only did none of them share my age, but we also had very little in common. Still, I learned that relationships form around one strong passion, in this case, soccer. After high school, these skills will help me find a diverse friend group because we'll all be moving into adulthood together. While freshman year included plenty of hard work, I like to think that the strong bonds aided the Oregon 3A State Championship win that very year.

Sprawled over the turf that day, I looked up as a hand reached down and helped me to my feet. This support arrived when I needed it most, not only helping me up that day, but also becoming the catalyst for creating the leader I am today. I've even grown a few inches since then, making practices physically easier, but the biggest change is that I am now the captain the young freshmen aspire to become. And, the evolution of my dad's motto is just the thing to take with me as I leave home.

Davis

Davis studies economics at Willamette University, distinguished as one of forty-four schools in *Colleges That Change Lives* by Loren Pope. He says he loves the way economics can predict human behavior and even humanize data. As a senior, he plans to attend graduate school at the University of British Columbia to study economics and development. Davis advises college freshman to open themselves up socially in their first year, as "just having one good friend can change everything about your experience." Like other writers, Davis shows us how to take a meaningful moment from our lives and find the drama. His childhood fear of trying new things adds complexity to his essay, as his experience shows him the other side of failure: stretching yourself and finding success.

TICKET TO RIDE

I fidgeted with the quarters in my pocket, ensuring I had each and every coin to make it across the city. The bus stopped, and I jammed the slippery, jittery coins down the slot and gave the driver a look I hoped said "I have done this a million times." With the bus's pneumatic hiss, my little bit of confidence left rushed out. I had never ridden the bus alone before, but the time had come to attempt it. I was eleven years old, my parents were at work, and I had to traverse Portland and cross the Willamette river to get to the dentist's office. The bus driver handed me a ticket, and I scuttled and stumbled as the bus jumped onto the road.

When I was younger I was afraid of trying new things for fear of making a mistake. When I was about seven years old, my dad and I drove to downtown Portland to return a pair of hiking boots, except my dad was unable to find a parking spot. So, this meant I was to follow my father's instructions exactly, while he drove around the block: take the shoebox, walk into the store, and return to the person behind the counter. Unsurprisingly, there were complications with the return and the employee began to hurl questions at me. I panicked and bolted from the store through a blur of tears, leaving behind my desire for a new experience.

Not only was I afraid of making mistakes, I was also a very forgetful child, leaving homework at school or leaving my schoolwork at home; there was always something forgotten or lost. The bus ride was the first time when my parents had asked me to do something of this magnitude where I did not, or could not, veto the idea. When I sat down on the bus and I realized that I had not forgotten anything, or left anything at home, I marveled at my ability to take care of myself. I decided that I was resourceful enough to handle everyday situations; I wasn't seven anymore and was plenty capable. As I watched the grand city roll by aboard the number 54 bus, I discovered confidence. After all, I was well on my way to doing more than surviving the ordeal. I had nailed it.

I hardly ever think about that day on the bus, probably because I don't take it anymore. I now drive a car. I wasn't thinking about it on the day I woke up at 1am to attempt to climb Mt. Hood with my dad or when we built a quadcopter together for a Physics' presentation. I wasn't exactly thinking about it on the day I flew a plane, but I sure experienced some of the same feelings, the fright of trying something new and the rush of confidence that came with success. However, I might be thinking about it next fall when I first walk onto a college campus, needing to find my classes and remembering how to make friends.

That fateful afternoon in the summer of 2008, I hopped off the bus and walked down the block towards the dentist's office breathing a sigh of relief. My parents asked me later that day how it went, and I played it cool, not making a big deal out of my bus adventure. I got over my fear of new experiences on that day and began calling them adventures instead of ordeals. It began the process of molding me into an independent young man who pursues life with a passion for learning new things and with the ability to put the reward of risking failure over the possible embarrassment that comes with first times.

Halle

Halle received admission at Brandeis University and Bates College, but chose Dickinson College in Carlisle, Pennsylvania, after receiving the John Dickenson Scholarship, a $20,000 annual award toward her tuition. She's since completed a semester abroad in Copenhagen and double majors in psychology and education administration, although she says her time abroad caused her to rethink her career goals. As a senior, she's opening up her possibilities inside of her majors to explore options including entrepreneurship. Halle's essay is an excellent example of what some writers call "exploding a moment," when she takes you inside the memory of her first babysitting adventure. She uses her experience to show us the origin of her love for children and education, as well as highlight her scientific mind.

BIG LESSONS, SMALL CHILDREN

At age fourteen, I cared about three things: clothes, coolness, and kids. But it wasn't until my first babysitting experience that my passion for children was tested.

"We're starving!" blurted the two shining faces staring up at me. "Then dinner time, it is!" I said with no hesitation. *I got this one in the bag! Making mac n cheese is totally easy.* I sauntered into the kitchen with four-year-old Calvin and seven-year-old Sophie, only to find a daunting old-fashioned gas stove staring me in the face. No touchscreen, no temperature gauge, just a single knob and burner. I flared up the gas, still hoping for an automatic flame to arise, but alas only the smell of rotten eggs burst from the burner. As I panicked, Sophie calmly sorted through the Tupperware while Calvin performed summersaults behind the counter. "Halle check me out!" he said as I discovered the lighter hiding in the drawer organizer. In one swift motion, I ignited the gas ring in an inferno of relief, and in eight short minutes, dinner was on the table. But more importantly, everyone was alive.

Before I started babysitting I called my little brother "my baby," essentially treating him as one of my life-sized dolls. Once I entered my preteen years, however, I craved something more than a falsified experience, so I obtained an oh-so-sophisticated babysitting license. In fact, this was the first thing I showed Calvin and Sophie's parents, Mr. and Mrs. Pectis, when I introduced myself on their doorstep. My time with the Pectis family marked an important transition. More than just a practical experience, it provided me with the realization that working with children is more than just play. This revelation led me down several different avenues involving work with children: two years working as a kindergarten teacher's assistant, counseling in summer camps, hosting daycare and birthday parties at the local community center, and volunteering with special needs children once a week at Bridlemile Elementary. Moreover, I have studied child and human development through AP Psychology and have been trained in child development by the learning specialist at Mary Reike Elementary.

From these experiences, I've discovered that I have the mind of a scientist. During my first time babysitting Calvin and Sophie, I identified distinct personality differences: Sophie was analytical and organized, while Calvin was a free-spirited ball of energy. That night I watched these personality differences manifest into their unique actions. Sophie helped calmly locate the lighter, while Calvin performed for my attention. This observation piqued my interest in relationships between the wiring of the brain and outward behavior, especially regarding the little people of the world.

The fact children are "little people" became important to me as well. Growing up, I hated nothing more than being talked down to. Even though I was small, I was still a human being with a spunky attitude. However, many people still elected to treat me, and many of the other little people of the world, like dolls. Today, I choose to treat everyone as an individual. Everyone, even the low-functioning special needs children I work with, deserves respect. Not granting this respect does them a disservice and inhibits growth.

As we allow children the freedom to grow, we grow as well. In working with kids since my very first babysitting job at 14, my views on both children and the direction I want to head in my own life have changed dramatically. I've discovered that aside from just loving kids, I'm an advocate for children and want to pursue child psychology. At seventeen, the three things I care about most include volunteering, learning, and kids. Clothes are still an honorable mention.

Samson

Samson was awarded the Summit Scholarship from the University of Oregon, where he plans to study mathematics and computer science. As a first-team, all-league 6A third baseman, Samson, like Ben, carefully weighed continuing with baseball at a smaller school with the attraction of a larger campus like U of O before making his final decision. This summer he interned at the Portland-based company Baseballism. At U of O, he sees himself participating in intramural sports, along with a challenging course load. Samson's essay takes a familiar topic—changing life directions—and shows us how to create an original and compelling essay out of the Common Application's "turning point" prompt. By connecting his experience to the present and future, Samson demonstrates the significance of a seemingly far-away time on our decisions today.

QUITTING ISN'T ALWAYS WHAT YOU THINK

The first practice of 7th-grade football season began at 10am in mid-August, two weeks before school started up again. Wearing a heavy helmet made my peripheral vision fuzzy, a familiar but uncomfortable feeling. It was a long day of drills and conditioning in the summer heat and coaches were eagerly watching for the fastest and strongest players. As the smallest on the team, I knew I must work harder for playing time this season. After five demanding hours of practice, my friends and I sprawled beneath the one shaded spot provided by a single tree. The coaches huddled, comparing players on their clipboards. I scrubbed the grass stains off my calves with my fingernails. I shook my one gallon water cooler, but it was empty. The next morning, I arrived again at 10am to see my teammates gearing up underneath the shade tree. But this time I walked past them, directly up to the coach, and handed him my helmet. I was quitting football.

Football was pivotal in my childhood. I spent years dogpiling with my friends on the hill during high school games, more hours playing catch on the playground during recess, and a lifetime of watching football on TV with family. I even dressed up as a zombie-football-player for Halloween three years in a row. That first practice of the year was different though, the people around me had grown while I had stayed small, and the game demanded a new level aggressiveness. When I took off my helmet and my vision cleared, I saw a multitude of new opportunities awaiting.

That fall I began my first semester in the select ensemble choir in middle school. I went from running around a field tackling friends to singing the tenor section of Christmas sheet music. I grew an interest in technology, began researching computers and how they work, eventually building my own out of parts I spent weeks collecting. Academics became more interesting. My seventh and eighth grade advanced math teacher Mr. Lang, famous throughout the school for his large ears and skillful nicknaming, inspired me to engage with math at a whole new level. Not only did I become mathematically interested, I began spending my free time learning about niche topics through documentaries, podcasts, and nonfiction novels. Not that I would ever need to know about how porta potties were invented, or how we are living in the sixth mass extinction on earth, but I uncovered a fondness for exploring these random topics.

Giving up football didn't mean I gave up athletics all together; instead I had more time to dedicate to baseball. The abilities required to be a good baseball player turned out to be in my skill set, much more so than football. Baseball is a sport where it doesn't matter where you come from and what your physical attributes are, but rather how hard you work and how focused you are. A common saying, and something that I truly believe, is that baseball is 80% mental. I played on the diamond in the spring, summer, and fall all the way through middle and high school. More important than the scores and the plays are my teammates. Together we battled Portland spring weather spending countless hours pouring dirt, raking, and weeding Clopton field so that we could play some ball. Transcending the long weekend trips and late night comebacks, my baseball community encouraged me to focus to be the best I can, not just as an athlete but as an individual.

Taking off my football helmet that final time was a bleak moment. I was never going to play again. What started as a tough decision, unfolded into a realization that sometimes I have to let go to see the alternatives clearly.

Nicole

Nicole's essay, featured in chapter 1, is a very special entry in *Write Big*. Nicole, a bright, passionate, caring, adventurous, and beloved student at the Robert D. Clark Honors College at the University of Oregon, passed away suddenly while I was writing this book. Our Southwest Portland community, along with the University of Oregon, feels the loss of Nicole deeply. In her short 19 years of life, she left an unmistakable impression on the world around her, and I feel so very fortunate to have known Nicole as a student and a friend of our family. Like so many students in this book, Nicole received impressive admissions into great schools like the University of Portland, Santa Clara University, and Reed College, but she was ultimately drawn to the prestigious Robert D. Clark Honors College because of the smaller discussion-based classes. As a high school scholar-athlete, National Honors Society member, and independent traveler, Nicole believed in working and playing hard. She was especially proud of her work with U of O's Safe Ride program, a sexual-assault prevention service. Her essay highlights the origin of her love of travel, as Nicole had recently returned from traveling abroad in Europe and spending time with friends prior to her death in a skiing accident. Her family takes solace knowing Nicole left this world doing something she loved most. I couldn't imagine *Write Big* without Nicole's essay, as she truly embodies the spirit that the "future is now" and shows us how to live life to its fullest while we can.

A WHOLE NEW WORLD

I am going to tell you a little secret. I have assassinated kings, traveled to distant planets, panned for gold, and lived as a pet dog. Of course having parents die again and again is exhausting; thankfully I have only lived as these characters through inked pages. Books are the adventure that takes no preparation or prior knowledge--just a simple flip of the page. As Mason Cooley once said, "Reading gives us someplace to go when we have to stay where we are." Recently I grew tired of staying put. I was ready to write my own tale, and it couldn't be something as simple as fishing on a lake. My adventure had to be something worth writing about.

My storyline begins early freshman year. The following events occurred: my friend casually issued me an invitation to visit her in Finland; my parents nonchalantly said I could go on the condition I paid my way; I naively checked my savings and found it sorely depleted; I painstakingly proceeded to teach swim lessons for the next two years. Like a tick, I latched on to the idea that I could travel alone, abroad, amongst strangers.

Stranger ideas than traveling abroad had almost never crossed my mind. Growing up terrified of the city, I believed any trip to downtown Portland would end with me taken hostage or being orphaned. However, after attending school in the heart of downtown for three years and riding the city bus to and from school I had grown accustomed to the characters around me and was comfortable wherever I walked. I was glad to have grown more comfortable in the city environment when I was on a side trip to Norway when we miscalculated our train departure and were without parental guidance. We had to figure out on our own how to travel transcontinental that evening. Luckily I was confident in my problem solving capabilities and was at ease without transportation in a country whose language I did not speak . I was relaxed where and felt sure in my abilities to navigate my way home.

Thankfully, I was able to have these experiences and enjoy every minute of them; but last year solving my problems was not nearly as fun. Mid year I got sick and had to miss a large portion of the year. At the same time my father was in and out of the hospital due to medical issues. I got terribly behind in my work due to the overall outside distractions, and it was detrimental. However, I can see this as a good thing because I was forced to update my organizational skills and work habits which in turn made me a better student. Also, a story is not nearly as fun to read or experience if it is all smooth sailing.

My parents say that I can imagine new worlds and over exaggerate anything, but I can promise you that the skies in Finland are a much richer blue than I see in Portland and the soft greens that roam the countryside are much more friendly than the grass in my backyard. On the way to a cabin in the woods, we stopped by a castle that overlooked a lilypad infested lake. It was a medieval castle that was built entirely out of a yellow stone that had been put together in no particular order. I climbed my way to the king's chambers that overlooked the lake. I stuck my head out of a large door decorated in brass that led out into a courtyard, and for that moment, I didn't think about all of times I had lived as a queen. I was too amazed to be amongst such old walls and wondered what stories they had to tell.

Katie

Katie studies science, technology, and society at the University of Puget Sound, a college also featured in *Colleges that Change Lives*. After acceptances into Linfield College, Willamette University, Whitworth College, and Oregon State University, Katie chose UPS, located in Tacoma, Washington, because of their strong bio-ethics program, which has given her internship opportunities in the bioethics field. She was also awarded their Presidential Scholarship, renewable annually. Since starting college, Katie's added a religion minor, become chair of the student senate, and served as co-president of her school's bioethics club, paving the way for graduate school and a career as a bioethicist for an in-patient clinical hospital. She tells college-bound seniors to be unafraid to change their majors, as not only did she change hers three times but she learned too. Katie says, "You'll never know how fascinating a wildly unexpected subject is until you immerse yourself in it!" Katie's essay, like Birgitta's "Un Regalo" and Matthew's "Grocery Lessons," uses her drum-major ladder as an artifact to help demonstrate the importance of music in her life. Katie's essay also illustrates how to showcase critical thinking around ethereal concepts like music.

KATIE'S LADDER

Scribbled in small, messy handwriting on my ladder's back, right foot is my name: Katie Handick. Below it are the dates from all of my high school marching band competitions. And if you were to get down on one knee and lean in close, you would see "October 25th, 2014," as the last date written.

October 25th was a day I learned a valuable lesson, but not the one I expected. It was sunny and beautiful, and our show had never sounded better. As the head Drum Major of the Lincoln High School Cardinals, I walked the band to the stadium's entrance and led us in our competition ritual: the Cardinal Chant. Within the short span of two minutes, rain and wind replaced the sun and downpoured as we marched onto the field. Band members lost their hats, the color guard their flags, and the left goal post fell onto the turf with a thud all before we had begun. I hoped the show would be postponed, but my band director just shook his head. So I took a deep breath and ascended to the highest platform of my trusty ladder. It rocked from side to side, even as I was anchored by the directors sitting on the front and back. I gave the count-off, and we started the show.

I'd like to say we won that day, that we took home the giant trophy we'd long admired. This was the lesson I had expected to learn, that the hours and hours we had put into the show had paid off. However, when we lost-- by a lot-- I learned that while hard work doesn't always lead to victory, it can lead to other more profound insights about collaboration and, in this case, the beauty of music that I've fallen in love with.

In music, notes come together to give a visual representation of collaboration and unity, demonstrating the teamwork I witness from atop my ladder. As the Drum Major, I see that collaboration take physical form. That sense of synchronicity that transcends the care of winning or losing is what fuels my passion for this art. It is a degree of beauty that not even the audience can fully appreciate like the musicians can while immersed in the middle of it. This beauty is not diluted by a stormy failure of a performance, nor enhanced by a shiny 1st place trophy. It is a beautiful thing to recognize failure and keep trying anyway. While stepping back down my ladder would have been the easy path once I realized the conditions, climbing even higher yielded an entirely new experience, not bound by the need to win, but by pure passion instead.

As the wind blew sideways on that fall day, I saw my fellow band members through teary eyes and feared the worst: not just losing, but falling to my not-so-graceful death. But by the third movement I saw something that surprised me. The band members were laughing, as if they had never performed better in their lives. And in that moment I understood that while we'd never win, we were doing something that we loved, giving it everything we had, and that made all the difference. Interestingly, October 25, 2014 remains the last date on my ladder, something I couldn't have known as I climbed down at the end of the show.

I've stood on that ladder every Saturday for the last two years of my life. I've put in a calculated 492 hours of rehearsal plus practice outside of school. To think that the pinnacle of my high school band career would end in last place with wet hair might have made me sad once, but because of that performance I can confidently say that I've learned what it is to feel passion in its purest form.

PART III:
HEROIC TALES FROM COLLEGE-BOUND SENIORS

"One of the few things I know about writing is this:
spend it all, shoot it, play it, lose it, all, right away, every time...
give it, give it all, give it now."
— Annie Dillard

15

EVERYTHING + THE KITCHEN SINK
STORIES

Stephanie

Stephanie learned that Willamette University now teaches the expectations of a great college application essay based on "The Lego Story." After acceptances and substantial scholarship offers from Willamette and Whitman Universities, as well as acceptance at Scripps Research Institute, she ultimately chose her first-choice school, Smith College in Northampton, Massachusetts. She's looking ahead to a summer internship with an Oregon congressman and even farther ahead to law school after graduation. In the immediate future, Stephanie says she loves animals and plans to get a cat while in college. Her essay is featured throughout the book because of its surprising topic and sophisticated approach. The strength of Stephanie's essay comes from the way she illustrates innovation rather than explaining how she's an outside-the-box thinker. This difference between showing and telling marks many of the great essays in this collection.

THE LEGO STORY

The man is about to propose. It's going to be perfect.

He's figured it all out: the music, the lighting, the shiny golden ring, even the restaurant, Palais de l'Amour. He must make her say yes, because he has everything planned perfectly. Suddenly, he has a sharp vision of their wedding day-- she'll wear the dress sold in Clasco's Emporium down the street, beside Barney's Pet Shoppe. They will marry in Chesterfield's Town Hall, built in 1891, and the photographer will take pictures that will never be developed. But that's okay-- that's what happens when you're a lego.

I know what you're thinking: legos are simple blocks you played with as a child. Maybe you built a dysfunctional car or a staircase into the air; these are strange topics for a seventeen-year-old girl's college application. But this perspective shows only a partial view of legos. Nothing reveals this more than the intricate Lego Creator™ city block in my attic. Each citizen of this two-foot long town has a complex backstory-- a family, a house, a personality. But the best part? With legos, you are given creative license to change these things.

I discovered legos at a late age by most accounts. I wasn't a young child when I began to construct the first portion of Chesterfield. I was twelve. But I consider this a lucky break for me-- just when my friends were contemplating careers, getting serious about schoolwork, and growing up, I found something that reawakened the child within me. As my friends lost their creativity, mine grew.

Every new book of instructions presented challenges that could not be solved by asking the teacher or copying off the internet. When the rule book was wrong, I had to improvise. When the design was faulty, I decided to change it. Sometimes I utilized my experience to reconstruct a defective window, door, or even an entire floor plan. Sometimes I added flourishes to buildings of my own accord or furniture where there was none. While in class, I learned to color inside the lines (or, rather, build inside the lines); at home, I was free to construct or change whatever my mind desired.

Take the man in the restaurant, about to propose. Strip away his shiny ring. Bring him outside the building, on his knees, arms outstretched. Now he is a beggar, holding out a plastic cup in hopes someone will donate to the cause. Or, move him up several stories, above the restaurant, into the apartment. Here he creates masterpieces of artwork, which are sold all over town. One even hangs in the mayor's office. Through what some would call play, I learned innovation, creativity, and just a little bit of rule breaking-- because when I changed the job or position of the characters, I went against the rulebook that demanded they stay put.

There are other rulebooks in life that have challenged me to innovate in ways I never imagined. For two summers, I taught kids of all ages how to swim, according to a 200+ page manual. "What do I do with it?" I remember asking. "You read it," my manager told me. "And then you memorize it." She then informed me a new manual would be issued every year. I learned very quickly that the rulebook was incomplete, failing to cover challenging scenarios. When a child in my class was an adept swimmer, but a poor listener, the book demanded I pass him. I realized that following the manual was not only wrong, but could actually put a child in danger.

As I gained confidence in my teaching style and myself, I realized that no matter how many manuals life hands me, they cannot tell me everything. Sometimes, life requires you to build outside the box. What started with legos blossomed into a different way to look at the world-- through a window tinted with creativity.

Sarah B.

After impressive acceptances from Gonzaga, Chapman, USC, Pepperdine, and Villanova universities, Sarah ultimately chose to study neuroscience and Spanish in Santa Clara University's Honors Program, where she received a scholarship as a Provost Scholar. She's served as a Christian diversity intern, community council president, and chemistry tutor. She has also been selected for the university emergency medical technician (EMT) training program and the Global Medical Brigades' Nicaragua team. Her advice for college-bound students mirrors the beliefs she took with her to Santa Clara: prioritize and stay present. According to Sarah, there's not enough time to do everything you want and time is too precious to waste on things that don't really matter. As you'll see, Sarah's essay addresses this very topic, as she selected one of the rarer choices from the Common Application prompts: solving a problem. A hallmark of Sarah's essay features her time markers and hour references throughout, but her topic alone showcases brilliance, as solving the riddle of twenty-four hours in a day isn't really something that can be done—unless, as Sarah shows us, you change the way you think.

THE 24-HOUR RIDDLE

Sarah attends school for 7 hours a day. Her teachers assign 2 hours of homework nightly for each of her 4 courses. Sarah's doctor prescribes 8 hours of sleep in order for her to be healthy. But dance rehearsal adds 1 hour to each school day, not including drive time. There are only 24 hours in each day, but student government, community service, and youth group can add at least 1 more hour to any given day. Sarah must still include: 1.5 hours for eating, at least 1 hour with family and friends, and 30 minutes for personal hygiene. Never mind if Sarah's grandparents stop by. What should Sarah subtract? How will she decide?

6:09 AM: the exact minute my alarm has been sounding for the past six years. During this time, I have been following the prescription for being a good kid, reaching higher than the standards expected of a teenage girl, and chasing after personal passions while balancing my life as a student. At some point, however, I began to question the writers of this math problem. In calculus, we call this type of dilemma "the solution does not exist." Yet, most *successful* people are constantly juggling family, work, and school, while solving world hunger on the side. American culture glorifies busy.

1:00 PM: the hour for la siesta in Ciudad Darío, Nicaragua. The shops are closed. Children are all home from school. And the streets and market are quiet. For the ten days I spent in Nicaragua, the village remained still for this hour. My group left our worksite, bumped away in the back of a pick-up truck, and waved to the dozen, giggling children along the road. We dropped our exhausted bodies into the comfort of hammocks lining the front of our home, while Izayana, the loving mother of the group, sat out on the porch. Izayana's laughter filled the air as she asked us questions about the day. Some people dozed off into an afternoon nap. I strummed songs on my ukulele. Whether one slept, talked, or played, la siesta provided an opportunity to rest.

8:00 PM: the time my plane arrived home in Portland, Oregon. The nine hours spent on my flight gave me time to reflect and revealed the juxtaposition of the bustling international airlines and the small village in Nicaragua, the juxtaposition of busyness and rest. I began to inspect the way I spent my time: I crammed enough stuff into my day to fill the social prescription for success.

There are no siestas in the United States. Instead there are college application deadlines, activities, and homework. One cannot do all of these things and spend time with their family and friends. No matter how hard I tried, I could never do everything 100%. And important pieces kept falling through the cracks. Something didn't add up. It was time for me to change the math problem. When I subtracted less meaningful activities, I gained

214

time. In a way, it was an "addition." Moreover, I realized I could create my own siesta not by removing an hour a day, but rather by including a day of rest in my week. Now I take each Sunday to spend time with my family and friends and seek rest and quiet. I'm excited to take this new strategy with me to college when the slate is wiped clean, and I will get to select new ways to use my time. Adding this variable to my life equation has really helped me create a fuller life rather than having a life that is just full.

Birgitta

Birgitta received acceptance into all five of her colleges, including a $24,000 scholarship to Oregon State Honors college toward her four-year degree. She also received the Presidential Scholarship at the University of Vermont, funding $18,000 annually of her undergraduate education and $21,000 scholarship offers from the University of Denver and the University of San Diego. In addition to her acceptance at Gonzaga University and earning the Regence Merit award, a $19,000 annual scholarship, Birgitta used the lessons from *Write Big* to apply and win the Joseph M. Caltado scholarship, an additional $5,000 annual award at Gonzaga. However, the east coast stole Birgitta's heart, and she ultimately chose the University of Vermont in Burlington, where she plans to follow a pre-medicine track, to minor in studio art, and perhaps even someday run a company. This is no surprise to her family who've nicknamed her the "CEO." While the internships and natural beauty of Vermont drew her to visit the university, she adds that college tours provide equally impressive trivia and advises college-bound students to listen up. How else will they learn things like the invention of the sports bra in UV's theatre department, one of Birgitta's new and favorite facts? Birgitta's essay is a model for how to merge a full resume of interests and accomplishments into the college application essay. In her case, she uses an artifact—a little girl's bow—to foreshadow her values, while also introducing her love of documentary and passion for social justice.

UN REGALO

In two hundred years, if archaeologists were to investigate my desk, they would have no questions about the purpose of most items. There are pens for writing, lamps for working in the dark, journals for making notes, and other artifacts that tell the story of a devoted senior. Yet one item would surprise them. On my desk also sits a little girl's bow. Archaeologists might detail the plastic gems or theorize my favorite color was red but soon their calculations would reveal an important fact: the bow is too young for a girl in high school. And without asking me, the true purpose of the hair ribbon would remain a mystery.

Archeologists aren't the only people who explore human mysteries, but also documentarians who use artifacts and living people to explore human connection. If a documentary filmmaker wondered about the story behind the bow, they could simply ask me. For the last year, documentary films have been my guilty pleasure. I've seen films like *Casting Jonbenet* and *Life Below Zero*. I've even discovered most films can be organized into two types: filmmakers who observe the action and filmmakers who are fully engaged in it. But more than anything, a tour of documentary films highlights humans' divergent pathways and surprising unions.

In fifth grade, I created a timeline of my future based on the path my parents had taken. My parents had graduated college and gone to medical school at 22, married at 28, and had their first child at 30. At ten years old, this sounded like the perfect plan. Back then, I had never heard of films like *The Great Human Odyssey*. Yet this documentary highlights the multiple routes humans have taken and survived for thousands of years, not one perfect plan. For example, the filmmakers follow tribes from Africa to Alaska documenting how they not only changed over time and distance, but also carried out the same traditions and insights. When I made that timeline, I saw myself simply as a part of my family's story, but watching *The Great Human Odyssey* showed me my history is also part of the human story.

Today I would consider my story incomplete without my own experience traveling to a foreign country. It was like starring in my own documentary. In Ciudad Dario, Nicaragua I spent eight days hand-mixing cement, carrying bricks with children, and building a school. I felt like Gordon Buchanan, the documentary filmmaker, who spends three weeks living with indigenous tribes in his series called *Tribes, Animals, and Me.* Unlike the scientific approach of *The Human Odyssey*, this film celebrates human connection as each tribe embraces Gordon, and he earns their trust in less than a week. Earning someone's trust quickly was once something I only thought possible on TV, but when a woman from the community invited us to cook in her outdoor kitchen I felt like family. Prior to my trip, I assumed the key to trust was time, but I realize now that trust can be developed quickly from the simplest of things: fumbling through Spanish, sifting gravel in the grueling heat, and sharing fresh watermelon at the end of each day.

If a documentary filmmaker asked me why I kept the bow on my desk, I would tell a story about a lonely little girl named Rosa. And how in Nicaragua, we sang and danced at the closing ceremony. Rosa had a lazy eye and none of the other children danced with her, so I invited her to dance with me. When I said good-bye, she took down one of her matching, sparkly bows and handed it to me. When I tried to return it, she refused, telling me it was *un regalo*, a gift for me. Today, I keep it on my desk to remind me of the connection I felt with her, the connection that's possible even among strangers.

Elijah

Elijah's meditative essay got the attention of the dean of admissions at Marquette University, who wrote Elijah to praise his thoughtful essay. With scholarship offers from Marquette University Honors Program offering him $24,000 annually, Tulane University granting him $27,000 annually, and acceptances into American University and Northeastern University, among others, Elijah's hard work granted him a menu of great options. Although Elijah admits it was a tough decision between the balmy climate and vibrant culture of New Orleans and the metropolis of Washington D.C., he ultimately chose American University who awarded him a $15,000 annual merit scholarship. As an award-winning debater, recently winning a $1,000 scholarship in the impromptu speech category from a Linfield College competition, his parents say Elijah's multiple acceptances made college a hard decision for him due to his seemingly endless capacity to see all sides to an issue. At American, Elijah plans to study political science and economics and eventually study abroad.

PHILOSOPHY TALK

Who's your favorite philosopher? Nietzsche? Camus? Kierkegaard? While metaphysics is not exactly a popular topic amongst most teenagers, the circles I run in aren't often characterized as "popular." My answer: Dan Harmon, writer and creator of the hit shows *Community* and *Rick and Morty*.

I first developed an obsession with the creative works of Harmon in the summer prior to my seventh- grade-year. Whereas most kids would have been shooting hoops, slurping down ice cream, or basking in the sun, I stayed cooped up in my basement, spread-eagle on our sofa, eyes glued to the television. My first episode of *Community* came on a typical Portland, Oregon summer afternoon: overcast and 65. I was immediately enamored of it, and, like any teen preparing for a 5-season binge, I thought to myself, "Why not?" A seemingly innocuous question that I would later realize to be my jumping off point into the absurd. Delving deeper, in 2015, I found *Rick and Morty*, Harmon and Justin Roiland's chaotic world of absurdist and nihilist philosophies saturated in unfettered pessimism.

Pessimism should not be confused for nihilism. Pessimists perceive existence as emotional tragedy. Nihilists perceive existence as devoid of any intrinsic meaning. Absurdism adds a condition, saying: if there is no meaning, how can we value one meaningless thing over another? For

Camus, this meant laughter and sunsets took precedent. For Harmon, this means pickle-people and alcoholism. For me, this means randomness, satire, and a thirst for knowledge. How does Harmon channel his absurdism? Let's take a look into the chaotic world of *Rick and Morty*.

"Nobody exists on purpose, nobody belongs anywhere, everybody's going to die. Come watch TV." These are the words of comfort Morty imparts upon his sister. As the show's absurdist hero, Morty takes comfort and finds joy in the meaninglessness around him. On the other hand, when the world ends in a global pandemic and Rick and Morty flee to an alternate reality, Rick grabs a beer from the fridge and drapes himself across the sofa, completely unmoved by this experience. As the show's pessimistic nihilist, Rick numbs himself to his pain that the world has no intrinsic meaning or value. Through *Rick and Morty*, Harmon offers his viewers two options: existence can be pain if you let it or bliss if you embrace it.

Their world is far removed from mine, but the lesson still translates. *Rick and Morty* fostered a jumping off point for my own ontological introspection, and I began to rethink what I want out of life. Since seventh grade, a lot's changed. I'm no longer that lonely kid, cooped up in his basement. I've moved to my room. My younger self sought material wealth. Profit supplanted my happiness. After considering absurdism, I realized there's no reason for me to pursue money and a 70-hour work week if it'll make me unhappy. This paradigm shift has driven me to pursue an intellectually rich life. It's why I debate. It gives me an opportunity to explore profound ideas in an intellectual community. It's why I write music. It provides a creative outlet that pushes me beyond my self-perceived limitations. It's why I pursue Economics and Political Science. I seek to better comprehend what drives the world around me. Each lens is an insight into the enigma of life and that search is fulfilling.

We can wallow in the pain of a universe indifferent to us. We can allow it to corrupt our thought and derail our pursuits. We can try and numb ourselves to our realities. Or, we can be active participants in our own lives. We can pursue the things we love. Given Harmon's dichotomy, I choose to embrace life in all its absurdity.

Bailey

Bailey received admission from notable schools nationwide, including acceptances from Fordham, Northeastern, and Boston Universities, along with admission into top west coast schools such as Chapman University, Loyola Marymount, University of California at San Diego, and the University of San Diego. Ultimately, she chose the suburban campus of Chapman University, in Orange, California, who gave her a $16,000 annual merit scholarship. After touring colleges around the nation, choosing Chapman came down to the bright connection she felt with the environment and people on the campus. Although she began college undecided, Bailey quickly fell in love with the film school and is earning a BFA in Creative Producing with exciting plans to direct feature length films and television shows. She's also leaning toward entrepreneurship and starting her own professional event planning business, catering to large scale events. Additionally, Bailey recently completed an interim course in London through Chapman, where she and twenty-eight classmates studied the role of race, gender, and identity in the novels of Harry Potter. Bailey's advice to college students is a testament to her initial opinion of the Chapman campus, "Pick a place where you want to spend the best four years of your life. And don't forget to call mom once in a while!" Bailey's topic is a great example of how our most meaningful experiences can be found sometimes among the moments colleges may never hear about from our list of accomplishments—a powerful reminder that wisdom comes from unlikely places.

BABY, YOU'RE A FIREWORK

There are few words to describe the euphoria, the god-like sensation, of a warm spotlight shining directly on you. Stage presence has always come naturally to me, but I never expected it would come in handy for a job. Last June, instead of a stage I was standing in the middle of a parking lot at the Washington State Fairground, full of nervous people, sitting in camping chairs, waiting to hear their names called. My new friend Julie wished me luck. A stern woman faced me, sized me up, and mechanically told me the name of the firework to demonstrate. I took my place in the center of the asphalt and announced to the crowd I would be performing "Shining Starlight." I knew my job was to impress the judges by using exciting adjectives and making a boring firework come to life. The stakes were high. I heard the bang, watched the sparks fly, and instantly began translating the firework display into language and absurd hand gestures: HULK GREEN, FAIRY DUST, LAVENDER STROBE LIGHTS, PYROTECNIC GEL, AND RICE CRISPIES POPPING. It was the longest 20 seconds of my life.

For seven days in July 2015, I worked at the biggest firework tent in the United States. I had been going to the TNT Firework Warehouse in Vancouver, WA since I was a kid. Morning glories, pagoda boxes, pink diamonds, and smoke grenades were some of my childhood favorites. When I returned at 17 it wasn't because I needed the money but because I loved the fourth of July. Also, I wanted a job that would incorporate a passionate interest. However, I underestimated the difficulty in getting the job at TNT. Out of the 100 people who auditioned for Firework Sales Associate, only 50 got the job. I knew I would be learning sales tactics from TNT, but what I didn't know was there would be unintended lessons inside of those very techniques.

Sales Lesson 1: The Sacrificial Lamb

The sacrificial lamb technique is all about earning the customer's trust. For example, our managers taught us to never say that a firework was bad, but if a customer hadn't seen it before we were supposed to tell them how it wasn't a great firework. However, the "sacrificial lamb" became more of a crutch for me than a useful tool. Quickly, I learned that telling a few jokes, kindness, and conversing with the customer was much better for gaining trust. In the end, I valued authenticity over being a top-seller. Interestingly, by July 4th I was the best seller at TNT.

Sales Lesson 2: Every firework is a good firework

Our managers taught us that every firework has a distinct quality. In other words, we couldn't claim that one firework was the best because that would make the other fireworks seem less impressive. Even our "sacrificial lamb" wasn't a bad firework. This lesson reminded me of something my mom has always taught me, "Every person has a special quality that makes them unique." This simple philosophy has taught me to look for the good in everyone, my own kind of optimism. This quality made selling fireworks in 100-degree weather a lot easier.

Sales Lesson 3: Uno Mas

The uno mas rule states: always try to sell one more. If we could accomplish this strategy with every customer, then hundreds of more fireworks would eventually be sold. This rule taught me two things. One: small things add up. Two: be persistent. My dad has always told me, "be aggressive" and "follow up," and yet somehow when the lesson became useful and immediate, his wisdom finally made sense.

I'm sure TNT never intended to teach me these life lessons. During auditions I questioned why I was driving 90 minutes to a dinky job at a firework tent. Now, however, I realize along with accomplishing my first job, I have real world experience, refined people skills, and confidence that I can succeed in the future, not to mention I am the best Piccolo Pete whistler in the Pacific Northwest.

Emma

Emma is an award-winning artist who recently won the Gold Key Award for her visual art portfolio submission to the Oregon Scholastic Art and

Writing Competition. Her work will be entered into a national contest, giving her the opportunity to win a $10,000 scholarship. Additionally, Emma received a $24,000 scholarship offer from the University of Oregon and a $75,000 four-year offer from the School of the Art Institute in Chicago. With acceptances into the Virginia Commonwealth University School of the Arts, Hampshire College, Tufts University, and Sarah Lawrence College, Emma decided on a liberal arts education in Bronxville, New York, through Sarah Lawrence. As an accomplished artist and musician, she notes her career path will likely include art and design but she is open to a career in science, a subject she also enjoys. Emma selected Sarah Lawrence because of what she wants from a college experience: great discussions with her classmates and teachers, training for solving difficult problems and thinking critically, instruction in writing improvement, and opportunities to study abroad and create great art. Emma says she also wants to develop strong friendships and become more independent. Her essay draws us into a powerful musical performance and explores the discipline of becoming a dedicated musician. Her critical development shows colleges her fearlessness, curiosity, and willingness to work hard for her dreams.

SHOSTAKOVICH 10

Every member of the orchestra is fully concentrated and my eyes are glued to Larry Johnson's baton as it cuts through the air. *One two, two two, three two, four two.* I count in my head the beginning of Shostakovich's tenth symphony, movement number two: *Stalin.* Sitting up straight at the end of my chair, I inhale. *Five two, six two.* The bursting sound of four clarinets erupt through the string's unremitting beats with eerie clarity, screaming a depiction of Stalin himself. A furious military snare-drum marches through the frenzy and leads to wails of cellos. As the music intensifies, the collective energy of the orchestra releases my mind from reading notes and an overwhelming feeling of joy and fulfillment replaces my concentration.

Some moments in music are extraordinary, like the night I played Shostakovich with the Portland Youth Conservatory Orchestra. But most of them have been ordinary, like all of the nights I spent practicing clarinet on the edge of my bed. I chose this instrument in fourth grade, simply because my mom's plastic clarinet had been collecting dust in our basement for the last thirty years. So, when in 6th grade, my clarinet teacher suggested that I audition for the Portland Youth Philharmonic, I thought *why me?* But as a shy twelve-year-old, I nervously auditioned, playing the piece *Chrysalis* by Gustave Langenus, and to my surprise was accepted into the beginning wind ensemble. I felt like I had been chosen to play in the *Hunger Games*.

During the following four years in this organization, I realized that fear could only be replaced with hard work. For instance, my conductor Larry Johnson constantly told the clarinet section to play louder. "Put your bells over your stands if you have to!" But, I learned that I could only achieve the confidence to play loudly if I knew my part, and that meant practicing it at home. So, in addition to exploring Portland's thrift stores with friends, doing homework, and devoting myself to art, I learned challenging symphonies like Rachmaninoff 2, Bruckner 8, and Shostakovich 10. I took the ambition that others had for me and used it as fuel to accomplish more than I believed was possible.

An ambitious clarinet student soon learns that you need tenacity to overcome the multitude of obstacles in musical education. The first is counting. *One two.* Then there are scales. *Two two.* Next, there's articulation. *Three two.* And finally, there's embouchure. *Four two.* This list makes learning an instrument seem simple, but the more advanced you become, the more obstacles you encounter. The time I learned how to play altissimo (really high) notes was like trying to get to the top of a climbing wall with loose pegs. At the beginning, my nightly practices were only screeching squeaks. I felt bad for my neighbors. But with continued effort, breakthroughs did happen. It took me years of failure to discover and memorize how to form my embouchure for each note, to recognize each intonation, and control my articulation perfectly. Of course, I still make mistakes, but it's just part of my learning process.

Experiencing breakthroughs as a result of practice has given me the necessary confidence for setting high standards and goals for myself. When I first joined the youth wind ensemble, I knew very little of persistence, and I certainly never thought I could make it to PYP's renowned philharmonic. However, now I'm proud to have experienced extraordinary moments while playing music with others, to have seen Larry's look of satisfaction after gaining the confidence to play loudly, and to have progressed into the top philharmonic after years of dedication and hard work. Enduring through the challenges of playing an instrument has made me brave and desirous to achieve what seems impossible.

Zane

When I first met Zane, he wasn't sure his life was interesting enough for a personal essay. Like Stephanie from "The Lego Story," he thought of himself as somewhat boring. However, if you read his enchanting essay, you'll feel drawn into the Led Zeppelin song detailed in his SIDE DOOR ENTRANCE. How did he come up with such a great topic? Zane began to think about a favorite place, per one of the old prompts on the Common Application. Soon he realized the location (like Shaina who writes the following essay) was unconventional: sitting on the edge of his bed playing guitar. The backstory about this quiet spot in his home gives the essay context and richness, while the description of the song illustrates the way music can transport us somewhere else. Zane studies computer and information science at the University of Oregon, home of the Ducks.

RAMBLE ON

Led Zeppelin's "Ramble On" opens with a simple chimy E major chord, wispy like the wind. Although the beginning is relaxing and blissful, the song turns to Led Zeppelin's signature hard rock style by the time the chorus comes. Listening to the song is like an adventure. As I later discovered, Led Zeppelin wrote the song about *The Lord of the Rings Trilogy*, one of the greatest adventure stories of the twentieth century. At only thirteeen, I sat on my bed and held my guitar in my lap, ready to begin. Surprisingly, the sound was not even remotely similar to the actual song, but I still look back to that moment as the beginning of my own journey and all that I am capable of now.

Since I was thirteen years old, the location where I play guitar has shifted from the edge of my bed to a collapsed, ugly couch, but the act of playing music has become a solitary activity where I can be completely focused and content. Music was once a mysterious thing I felt unable to comprehend. Although I listened to music daily, I had no idea how it worked, much like how most people do not understand how the cars they drive work. I wanted to dissect songs, to examine their unique structures. Having recently moved in with my mom's boyfriend and his three sons, there were very few things that were truly my own. But my guitar and my music were mine, and no one else's.

Playing guitar provided me with a valuable lesson: talent is important, but persistence is just as critical. When I first began playing, playing even simple songs proved to be no easy feat. It was as if I had been thrown into a foreign country, and I didn't know the native language. Incorrect notes were common, and nothing ever sounded the way I intended. It may have been clumsy and awkward, but eventually, it all came together. Simple notes became chords and chords became simple melodies; what was once a disjointed tune was now a euphonic song, not because it sounded perfect, but because it was created by me.

Music demands thinking outside the box or, as psychologists call it, divergent thinking. Recognizing multiple solutions to the same problem develops over time. I may have been able to speak the language of this foreign land, but with a heavy accent. Songs sounded stiff, forced, and artificial. Often times, the most obvious way to play a song was not the best way to play it. I soon realized that one had to adapt to the style of each song. It had to sound natural, and it was the small, obscure touches that perfected the sound. Not surprisingly, divergent thinking is also applicable to real-world problems outside of music. In computer science, one is presented with a problem and is tasked with finding the most efficient way to solve that problem. Both the musician and the computer scientist must be capable of recognizing the less obvious of these solutions and putting them into practice.

Today when I sit down and play my guitar, I often remember when I first tried to play "Ramble On." As it turns out, the way I first played it was not the best way to do so. As I have gotten better at recognizing the more obscure solutions to problems over these last five years, I have improved my version of "Ramble On." Although it may not have the same sound as the studio recording, my version has some of the charm of the original. When I finally make my way to college, I won't have my own space anymore. Instead of four brothers, I'll have many roommates. My old room will be left behind, but I will still have my guitar, and I will be bringing music--and all I've learned--with me.

Shaina

Shaina studies biology at Grinnell College in Grinnell, Iowa, where she received the Trustee Scholarship. Grinnell College is routinely ranked one of the best liberal arts colleges in the nation, with U.S. News and World Report listing it as number eighteen in the country for National Liberal Arts Colleges. More than their rankings, Grinnell's 9:1 student to teacher ratio is a key factor that draws students like Shaina from across the U.S. Shaina says she hopes to attend graduate school after she completes her undergrad studies but would like to work for a few years first in her field. Her essay takes an older prompt from the Common Application—a favorite place— and innovates on the concept, as Shaina's favorite place is a moving city bus. Her approach shows us the elasticity of the Common Application prompts, much like Sarah's essay on twenty-four hours in a day. Even though the current Common Application prompts do not include the "favorite place" option, Shaina could still write this exact essay today by selecting the "choose your own topic" option.

EN ROUTE

It begins with the walk, normally done at a brisk pace because I am often late. As I approach the bus stop, my ears listen for the subtle purr of the engine. This day, as with most, I arrive just as the bus rounds the corner. As I hurry across the street, the vibrant reds and oranges fill the sky. The bus pulls up and stops; it almost seems to exhale as the doors open, inviting me inside. I take my first step, flash a good morning at the driver, and then begin the meticulous process of choosing a seat. My favorite seat is up the step on the left because it allows for the best view of the city, and fortunately it's open. I take a seat. The bus now pulls away from the stop almost gliding on the slick city streets.

I have been taking the bus to school for seven years. It began out of necessity, but became a welcomed ritual. In everyday life, you are constantly moving and watching everything else stay still. On the bus, you are still while everything else is perpetually in motion. I like to observe. When I sit on the bus I feel perfectly content. I don't think much, instead I absorb.

We roll up to our first stop, in front of my old elementary school, Glencoe. The large e-shaped building surrounds the new plastic playground. The space consists of weathering foursquare courts and fraying basketball hoops. Continuing, the large grassy field opens up. You can barely make out the lines of the soccer field and the friendly posts of the goals, where I spent every recess. Unlike the other girls, who spent their time on the monkey bars, I played soccer instead. I would stand in the goal and watch the game unfold. I saw everything: the players running in and out, the games of tag in the background, and the teachers steadily walking back and forth.

My favorite part of the bus ride is crossing the Morrison Bridge. As we reach the crest, the city opens up outside the window. I put down whatever distraction is in my hands, my phone or notecards, and focus on the view. The sun glints off the mirrored surface of Big Pink, the tallest building in Portland. At this moment, almost on top of the world, the whole city seems to stop. Everyday life requires my unwavering attention to a single goal; however, to observe the world on the bus needs no singular attention.

As we enter downtown, the bus is cramped, with every seat and empty space occupied. People are constantly bumping into each other, jockeying for a position closest to an exit. In some ways, this scene parallels my life today. My life is crowded with deadlines and obligations: tests and projects for school, daily practice and games for soccer, and the pressure of finding a college. I am constantly in contact with the ideas and desires of other students, who like the people on the bus, are looking for an outlet. For a moment, the chaos is overwhelming, as an internal pressure builds, and there is a murmur of excitement as the stop nears.

Finally, we reach 5th and Washington, and I have the last five minutes to myself. My awareness shifts to the absence of bustling and tension. My exit approaches. The doors exhale open. I take a deep breath and step off the bus.

Makenna

Like many top high school athletes, Makenna wanted her college experience to include playing the sports she loved. When Linfield College, a small, private liberal arts college in McMinnville, Oregon, offered her a $16,000 annual merit aid scholarship and roles on their soccer and softball teams, her college search ended. At Linfield, Makenna majors in business with plans to study abroad next fall in Australia to advance her major. She gave up soccer after her freshman year but continues to play softball for the school, in addition to working at Linfield's Human Health Athletic Building. In spring 2018, Makenna won the "First Team All-Conference" recognition for the Wildcats. This hardworking student and athlete has some surprising advice for success in college: don't forget to have fun. And by fun, she means get out of your comfort zone, "College goes by fast. It's your last chance to have fun before the real world, so make the best of every opportunity and be open to trying new things." Makenna's essay is not only a tribute to her beloved softball but an exploration of the meaning of team and failure. Like Samson's "Quitting Isn't Always What You Think" and Dezi's "Never Count Anyone Out," her essay demonstrates how to write about sports in a fresh and interesting way.

THE UPSIDE OF FAILURE

Softball is a game of failure. There are the traditional errors: nine different variations, a failure for every single position on the field. And then there are the offensive mistakes: pop-out, ground-out, strike-out. In fact, a batter is more likely to get out than get a hit. Yet if she fails as much as 70-60% of the time, she is considered excellent.

In my 12 years of playing softball, I've learned a lot about failure and success. I have learned these lessons not alone, but as a part as a team. We win and lose as a team; no one wins or loses individually. In a game, I have teammates who perform well, and I have teammates who bat 0/4 while simultaneously making multiple errors. The mental aspect of the game will destroy us without the support of each other or without individual resiliency. In softball we have a unique language spoken between us; we have cheers for keeping the game simple and for being tough in the box. And we need these encouragements because when the opposing team takes the field, it's all about making us fail. Yet when we run to our positions, flanked out into the shape of a diamond, we are an army of nine against one.

See ball, hit ball.

This cheer is one of the most common yelled from the dugout to the batter. We remind our teammate not to outthink herself while standing in the box because this game isn't very complicated: see the ball, hit it, and run around the bases. Of course, technically speaking it's more complex, but when someone is in the box it's crucial to simplify everything. I learned this lesson myself over the summer by batting against one of the best pitchers at the Triple Crown National tournament in Reno, Nevada. I was batting third in the line-up, and the previous batters struck out swinging. I began to think: *stay calm, stand in the back of the box,* and *don't swing at anything above my eyes.* And then I heard my teammates cheering "See ball, hit ball." I closed my eyes and relaxed. It didn't matter what type of pitch she was going to throw me; I just needed to hit it. I stepped into the box, took a sharp swing, and hit a single, right up the middle.

Tough with two.

On offense we yell this to our batter when she has two strikes. All the pitcher needs to do is throw one more strike and you're out. To protect the plate, we must battle--to fight off every single pitch that could be called strike three. For me, nothing is more rewarding than getting on base after having two strikes against me. However, striking out is not the kind of failure I like learning from. I wish I could say I have accepted it, but I absolutely hate it. I feel obligated to put the ball in play, not only for me and my stats, but for my team. If I fail to do so, I feel as if I have let my team down. However, if I allow myself to get sucked into the negativity vortex, I will stay there. Even though being "tough with two" means battling at the plate, I can't always be victorious there. But the lesson that I'm learning at the plate is something I'm able to use anytime life calls for mental toughness.

Softball and sports are a huge part of my life; however, I'm smart enough to know that I can't play them forever. In the future, whether it's old age, an injury or sickness, I know my career will end. But the lessons about being a part of a team, overcoming failures and knowing that I have to be a fan of my best efforts are lessons that will continue far beyond my batting average.

Theo

Theo's topic is a meta-meditation on the Common Application prompt for a subject that makes one lose all track of time, as he chose to write about flow theory. Like many students, Theo wanted to combine many of his interests in the college application essay to create an engaging narrative. His philosophical essay helped earn his admission and receive an impressive $35,000 per year in scholarships to St. Paul Minnesota's Hamline University, consistently ranked one of the top schools in the Midwest. He will also be playing Division III soccer for Hamline's men's team and run track for the Pipers. As a competitive athlete, Theo plans to combine his interests by studying exercise science at Hamline.

FLOW

"Oh, we are definitely going to die!" one of my friends exclaimed as we hurtled straight towards a rock in the middle of the Deschutes river. My rafting group had chosen the hardest possible route in the whitewater. We were supposed to be navigating, as we had to pass through a tiny gap in the rocks in order to clear the massive rapid. But everyone was panicking, burrowing deeper into the boat in hopes that the raft wouldn't pop. Right before we reached the rapid, we all closed our eyes, rowing blindly with a last attempt to pass the rock. I opened mine to witness the boat jettison through the hole, past the obstacles, and back into the open river, and I felt utterly present, even happy, having experienced this life-or-death moment.

Flow, or focus, is a kind of tunnel vision. Yet, focused is not exactly a word I would use to describe myself when I was younger. For much of my childhood, I would characterize myself as a slightly aloof, goofy boy who was always worrying about the next thing. I had my interests but lived largely in a future world. This rafting trip occurred near the beginning of high school when I was maybe fifteen, and it taught me a very valuable lesson--that being present can save your life-but that's not its only gift.

One of the other gifts that comes from being present is known in psychology as the concept of a flow state. It's the condition that comes from feeling utterly immersed, or lost, in an activity. Everything- space, time, awareness of other people--falls away. Scientists believe that reaching this flow state many times is essential to living a long, happy, fulfilled life. My most meaningful experiences of flow occur while playing soccer. Sometimes I can achieve this during practices, but it's during games where the most powerful feelings of flow exist. Dribbling one-on-one with a defender, sprinting toward an opponent, and making a game-saving tackle are individual tests of strength and skill that make everything else fall away. Ironically, throughout most of my life, the commanding voices of society have taught me the opposite of flow- that success comes from logical and careful analysis, and that blanking out, relaxing, or letting go leads to failure.

One cannot live in a flow state all the time, but the wisdom of the flow state is this: we need both habit and flow, the unconscious and deeply conscious pieces of experience.

A related gift that comes from presence is not so much a flow state, but rather the fight-or-flight response, a heightened physical response that really makes people feel alive. In that raft, faced head-on with our potential doom, my body took over, and I was fighting for my life by paddling like I never had before. As a child, I would try to think and predict my way through everything. I believed that I could control all the variables and solve any problem through pure analysis. I didn't know about things like a flow state or the fight-or-flight response. Now, as I have begun to recognize that many unknowns exist, I have learned to trust myself. Some things can't be accomplished without both the body and the mind working together.

If we were to go back to that same river, and go down the same rapid again, I think I wouldn't be so worried about going down the dangerous, rocky route. I might even enjoy the risk! I would still be able to have fun and find pleasure in the moment, while giving some safety away to a big rock. That's the difference between a younger version of myself and where I am now. I'm ready to live in the moment, as I know that these risks and moments of presence and clarity are some of the most profound and important things in life. I've discovered new things about myself from experiences just like this, and even a few passions. I plan to continue the exploration of topics about the mind and body, such as psychology, kinesiology, and physical therapy. Until then, I plan on continuing my studies on the soccer field and out in nature.

Owen

Owen attends Willamette University in Salem, Oregon, where he received the Willamette and Jason Lee awards. At Willamette, Owen plays on the tennis team and studies film. Looking ahead, he plans to study abroad in Germany and perhaps finish his film degree at an institution that specializes in film studies. A gregarious and fun-loving high school student, Owen created an essay that showcases his natural ability to connect with others and his love of humor. His essay focuses on Nate, an autistic student at his school, and how their time together shaped his own world view. With a passion for film, Owen's essay illuminates Nate's world in cinematic detail.

NAKED MOLE RATS

When most kids go to the Zoo they want to see the lions and the bears and the elephants, but not Nate. Nate wanted to see the naked mole rats. Nate is a hefty seventeen-year-old with short brown hair who wears the same beat-up Nike sneakers to school, everyday. Nate goes to school like every kid, plays sports, and even goes to football games on Friday nights. Nate is a normal high schooler in every way but one. Nate has autism.

I'll never forget the first time I met Nate. I walked into room 142 and started my first class as a Special Education TA. I'd signed up to work with special education kids because I felt I had a knack for connecting with them. I knew that high school was tough for them socially, and I thought maybe I could help in some small way. The students were working

over math packets as I awkwardly introduced myself to the teachers, when Nate screamed "AHHHHH! He's gone savage!" and pointed at another boy in the room. Before I even said my name, the teachers sprung out of their seats and pried the student's hand from a different TA's hair, as I stood there in awe trying to remember where I had heard Nate's words before. As the teachers unhooked the student from the poor TA's hair I remembered: *Madagascar*! Nate has since gone on to quote countless other animated movies like this one, even going as far as to recite entire scenes.

Throughout the rest of that school year my connection with Nate grew, and he taught me some very valuable lessons about how to be myself. When I was a Freshman "being cool" was very important to me. Even though my mom called me her "social butterfly," I still wanted everyone to like me so I liked what everyone else liked. One day, during Special Education class all the students were doing an art project. Nate chose to use pink and purple markers for his picture, and almost immediately the boys in the class told him that those were girl colors. Nate just shrugged and said "No, they're my favorite colors." Nate helped me see that if YOU like something then it is cool. Who cares what anyone else thinks?

As I prepare for college, Nate's helped me realize the importance of knowing myself. To Nate, the colors were not simply uncool, they were his favorite. From my time with Nate, I noticed that he did not have the same struggles around balancing his favorite subjects, movies, colors, even mole rats, like some of my other friends. His example has encouraged me to not only like what I like, but to know what I like. I look forward to college because I think it can actually help me with this process of discovery.

The day Nate begged to see the naked mole rats, he had already tried to escape the group and go on his own. When we finally arrived at the exhibit he was beyond ecstatic, and he ran ahead of the group shouting, "This way to the naked mole rats!" Nate stood there with his face glued to the glass as he watched as the hairless rodents weaved their way through a series of tunnels. The rest of the class looked on, disgusted by the little, pink, ugly creatures. But not Nate. He was both amazed and fascinated. Nate saw the beauty and uniqueness of these pink rodents, and he showed me something else. Beauty can be found in anything, and we can all find happiness in the most unexpected places.

Dezi

For the last ten years, Dezi says nothing has been as consistent a force in his life as baseball. Like many high school athletes, he wanted to write about his beloved sport but did not want to submit an essay that sounded like a cliché. Dezi chose to open his essay with an inspirational story from a pivotal moment in his Little League career, when another player opened his eyes to the beauty of believing in others. His essay structure hinges on telling only half of the story in the introduction and the rest in his conclusion, a technique he used to stand apart from other essays about sports. He finished his final baseball season as the starting left fielder for his 6A high school team, as well as playing varsity soccer for his school. He plans to apply his love of athletics to pursue a degree in human physiology at the University of Oregon. Dezi was recently awarded first-team, all-league for the Portland Interscholastic League and listed as one of Oregon's top baseball players by *The Oregonian.*

NEVER COUNT ANYONE OUT

Parker was the kid on my baseball team who always batted at the bottom of the lineup. In little league baseball, the whole team hits, which means the worst batters go at the end. In other words, guys like Parker don't bat much. So, when it was the Southwest Portland Little League Championship, and our team, the Red Sox, were down by two against the Pirates, and Parker went up to the plate, I squeezed my bat as I watched from the dugout. It was the bottom of the sixth, two outs, runner on second, down by two. Our entire season was going to be decided in this one at bat.

At that point in my life, I'd been playing baseball for six years, but when you're twelve- years-old that feels like your whole life. I'd spent many days after school practicing with my team and countless hours in the backyard playing catch with my dad. On the night of the championship, it was a full count, and I was worried but not hopeless. My coaches had always told me that in baseball, you can never count anybody out.

A great coach can improve every player, but a bad coach only hurts the team. I've experienced both of these firsthand. For example, I went from being the MVP of my freshmen basketball team, to getting little playing time because the new coach decided that I wasn't part of his plan. The coach, a 40-something, short-tempered, hyper-competitive man, didn't even try to involve me in the team; we finished the season with a losing record. The record and the playing time was something everyone could see, but the toll it took on my self-belief was less visible. However, I've also learned that a good coach can take a team with a losing record and turn them into the number one team in the county. In eighth grade, Bruce and Andrew were twenty-something, fun loving, and competitive coaches that involved every player on the team. Bruce liked to say, "Adapt or die." Years later, I still remember his quote. If I struggle in my last at bat, I think about how to change my approach the next time, to improve my chances for getting on base.

What makes a team thrive is their chemistry; you can throw together a team with good players, but without good chemistry they won't succeed. Good teams have rituals. For instance, my baseball team last year decorated our locker room, bringing chairs, a mini- hoop, and doormats for our lockers. The locker room was like a second home, and my teammates were my family. The trust we establish off the field translates into the game when we make plays. However, one of my favorite baseball rituals occurs during game time, and it's called "baseball chatter." We have our own classic sayings like "Atta boy" and "Hum babe," along with our own like "You gotta put the toast in the toaster" for each batter. Baseball is stressful enough, so the goal is to relax the batter and have him loosen up during his at bat.

Today my friends and I haven't forgotten that moment when Parker batted during the championship. We were cheering, "Let's go Parker!" and "Get a base knock!" when suddenly the pitcher threw it high and outside, and Parker hit it over the right fielder's head, and it rolled to the fence, as our jaws dropped. Soon, Sammy, our third baseman, hit a double, and eventually it was my turn: a line drive up the middle. We won! We dogpiled Sammy, but after the game everyone agreed that we'd won the game because of Parker. Parker's story inspires me when I think about myself as a college freshman because soon I'll be the one out of place and inexperienced, but just like Parker, I'll get up there and give it my best shot.

Matt

As a writer, actor, and musician, Matt chose to extend his passions into his college major. He studies theatre arts at Southern Oregon University, in Ashland, home of the renowned Shakespeare Festival. His charming college application essay reads like a movie script of his background, interests, and vision as he explains the origin for writing a musical screenplay based on his grandmother's life. Like many students, Matt's essay meant more to him than his college application because it gave him a platform to narrate the power the arts and theatre community have had in his life. After he completes his undergraduate degree, Matt has big dreams of working on Broadway.

ARTISTIC LICENSE

Once, there was a young maiden who lived in the far off land of... Wisconsin. In the ancient time of... the 1940's. Her name was Mary Christine... Muchka. Everyone called her Chris. She was five when her father died, and her mother was left destitute with eight living children and a broken heart. But Chris was ambitious. She was resourceful. She was romantic. On summer nights she looked out the small window of her tiny Sheboygan home, facing downtown, and watched the parties on the rooftops. She dreamed herself into the parties where one day she would meet her one true love. During WWII, Chris was invited to a Naval Ball, where she arrived looking as stunning as ever...

Chris's story sounds like the beginning of a B-list romantic comedy, but it's actually the story of how my grandparents met. I added some artistic license, of course. Because that's what artists do. Truth be told, when I first heard my grandmother's story, I saw it set to a stage with lights, costumes, and original music. I stayed up for three months using all my spare time to write songs like "Cold Nights," "Rainstorm," and "Lost in Space." Let's just say I was going through a weather phase. Translating my grandmother's tales into musical scenes not only helped me resolve the conflict within the plot, but even the conflicting emotions within myself.

Nowadays I am an articulate and creative writer, but this was not always the case. When I was a young boy, like many children, I had emotions that were so intense I could not compress them into words. Instead, I would translate them into a song, which helped my parents and me because adding music resolved not just my feelings but created a bridge of understanding between us.

Today I write music for other reasons, but this early skill helped me understand the value of emotional content tied with self-expression. I needed this understanding when I wrote the play about my grandmother. For instance, when I imagined the setting for the original song "Rainstorm," I visualized the following: a strong woman finally at her breaking point, feeling there is no way out, the moment when she collapses, and the way her mother gently places both hands on her shoulders, comforting her as best she can. This moment is animated when the backdrop fades into darkness and a spotlight shines on the mother and daughter at center stage.

Unconditional love is something the drama community consistently demonstrated, ultimately instilling me with both self-confidence and perspective. This taught me to admire rather than fear the differences in people. In order to create great art you have to be willing to put your heart on your sleeve and show it to an audience. When everyone goes through this vulnerable process, it creates a sense of unrivaled community. As I look to college.

The story of how my grandparents met would be incomplete without telling you the following. When my grandpa first laid eyes on my grandma, she was flirting with another man. And initially, Grandma Chris found Grandpa Bob to be less than ideal looking. And when they danced, Grandpa Bob constantly stepped on Grandma Chris's toes. Through all this, however, they still fell in love. Their story reminds me that a full life creates a story worth telling, something that inspires me while I go off to create my own.

Preston

Preston received admission into all of his selected colleges with scholarship offers up to $20,000 per year. He began his college search reaching for schools outside of his GPA and test scores, working hard in hopes of receiving a menu of university options. His dedication to the application process paid dividends, with acceptances from the University of Montana, Montana State, University of Puget Sound, Pacific University, Oregon State University, Westminster College, and Western Washington University, among others. He ultimately chose Westminster College in Salt Lake City, Utah, a place where he can study business while also pursuing his passion of photography. Westminster also supports his love of the outdoors and dreams of being close to a mountain, as Preston believes his best college experience will be balanced with good snowboarding conditions. His essay, "Hell Day," takes a look at the lessons he gained from competitive swimming, even though he can no longer participate in the sport that once ruled his free time. "Hell Day" is an excellent example of demonstrating the awareness of crossover skills. With most students leaving a sport or commitment behind them in high school, the knowledge of valuable training applicable to future challenges is an impressive awareness to share with admissions counselors.

HELL DAY

Walking onto the heavily chlorinated deck, I knew that I was in over my head. Today was hell day, when our coaches required all swimmers to complete 3 insanely hard practices...on the same day. I knew that I could finish today, but at 5:30 am my real question was how am I going to get out of bed tomorrow? I took a couple of steps, jumped into the frigid water, straightened my swim cap, and took off.

Hell Day takes place on December 20th at the Multnomah Athletic Club, in Portland, Oregon, every year and consists of a total of 6-hours swimming in one day. In my swim career, I have attended 3 hell days, not to mention thousands of hours at practices and meets. I didn't swim hell day this year, or any other practices, because in 2016 I had to give up the sport I loved. This change was due to a respiratory condition, a reaction to chlorine and something my doctors still don't understand. I lost this passion at a really low point in my life, at a time when I questioned big things like my purpose or existence, small things like motivation, and other concepts that are harder to measure like being comfortable around people who were my friends. Today, I still don't have all the answers, but due to my disciplines in swimming and practices like hell day, I realize I have the ability to strive for more.

The Ultimate IM is the first out of the three practices on hell day, and it's all about technique and proficiency. This is where you swim a mile for each stroke in Individual Medley order, honing in on each stroke. For example, breathing is one of the more important aspects of swimming. To the non-swimmer it may seem as if you can breathe whenever you want, but actually there is a pattern. When I learned the butterfly, I used to take a breath every stroke. Practices like the IM allowed me to focus on breathing patterns, inherently making my time faster. Focusing on technique is also a great way to take the focus off of these big picture questions that overwhelm me. I've also learned that most people don't have these questions answered, no matter how old they are. While it's hard to turn off my mind, doing activities that require a lot of focus--driving, snowboarding, longboarding, or even calculus tests--provide a healthy distraction.

The second practice is the 101 100 meter freestyles (read as one-hundred and one, one hundred). The drill consists of beginning at one minute and thirty seconds, pyramiding down to fifty seconds, and finishing by building back up to 90 seconds, ending it at a total 101 100 meter freestyles. While it may seem that this practice all about speed, you actually learn how to take things at a much more manageable and accomplishable pace. Pace is something I've had to remember when going through life; I tend not to plan things out and live in the moment. Going through life at a very fast pace can lead to burnout, resulting in low motivation. From using a planner and defining routines, pacing myself has allowed me to still have the time to do activities, while also being able to get my work done on time.

The last practice is the jungle set. The entirety of this practice is how far can you make it within an hour and thirty minutes. This correlates to the notion that perfect practice makes perfect. If you continue with a sloppy technique in swimming, you can expect to repeat that sloppy performance in a competitive race. While if you fine tune it, making your technique the best it can possibly be, you commit that to your muscle memory. This can be applied not only to swimming, but how you treat yourself. Social situations are times when I'm faced with thoughts of self-degradation and self-loathing. It's taken practice to change this unhealthy mindset, but these lessons are especially helpful when it comes to calming myself down in times of stress. If you continue to demean yourself, this idea of imperfection is ingrained into your head; while if you look at your accomplishments, you will in turn view yourself in a positive light. This tactic has given me the endurance and/or will to meet new people and make connections in a social setting.

After stepping out of the pool soaking wet, the only thing I knew was that I was sore, able to go home, and had accomplished something important. Later on in my life, I began to realize that I gained more from these 3 intense practices than I originally thought. Formerly, I was planned on using the lessons from these practices in the pool. Now, as I leave home for college, I know I'll be applying the lessons of overcoming obstacles, pacing, and endurance to the real world.

ACKNOWLEDGEMENTS

"Generally, by the time you are Real, most of your hair has been loved off, and your eyes drop out and you get loose in the joints and very shabby. But these things don't matter at all, because once you are Real you can't be ugly, except to people who don't understand."
— Margery Williams Bianco, *The Velveteen Rabbit*

Write Big has definitely challenged me to become real. After years of teaching college writers and coaching students, the process of creating this book challenged me to step out and share my work. There are few things as intimidating as being a writing professional who is writing a book about writing—what if I get it wrong, what if I make a mistake, what if, what if, what if…

But ultimately I chose to take the very advice I've given my students: to become the protagonist of my own story. Sometimes it feels like a wobbly ledge and other times like a mountain top.

Atop the mountain, one is grateful. I would like to thank my loving friends and family who encouraged me to get this book into the world. Every bit of instruction and advice I give in these pages, as I was sometimes reminded of by them, became wisdom I needed to follow in order to complete *Write Big*.

I am indebted to my three sons, Chaz, Dezi, and Nico, who endured many late dinners and a mom with a very busy mind at all times. I have poured every hour into this book fueled by my love for you—thank you for your patience.

When I think of all the wisdom included here, I know I am sharing much of what has been passed down to me. In the spirit of helping high school students, I would like to thank three special high school teachers who helped me identify my love of language and story and encouraged me to follow my passion. Eleanor Hutto, my enthusiastic Spanish teacher who deepened my affection for language and culture, Jennifer Hauck, South Forsyth's illustrious French teacher and my mentor and coach, and Patti Smith, the English teacher who read poetry to us breathlessly and taught us what it meant to lose oneself in a story—to all of you, I am so grateful for my holistic education and for your belief in me as a student and as a person.

More recently, I would like to thank Dr. Deborah Barany, of Barany Educational Consulting. Dr. Barany is a dear friend and educator who has referred many of her students to me, where I've had the privilege of partnering with her as she guides college-bound seniors toward the pursuit of their dream colleges and universities. Many of the essays included here and the success of the students' admission is owed to her unique ability to match students to ideal institutions. Dr. Barany embodies the spirit of this book, a devoted educator who values the connection of personal fulfillment alongside educational achievement.

Additionally, I have been guided and supported by a tremendous business coach and mentor, Kyle Sexton, who has challenged and encouraged me to share my work with a wider audience. He is also the talented designer of *Write Big's* layout and book cover, as well as my Boxcar Writing Labs logo. His expertise was sought at every stage of this book, and my gratitude exceeds words—a rare occurrence—for his contributions. I can only say that I've placed it all carefully away in my locket.

I would also like to thank Michelle Blair, my editor. Her contribution to *Write Big* has ensured the quality of story and instruction I wanted to share with college-bound seniors is clear, consistent, and concise. I am so grateful to her every note, question, and comment that advanced the message of this book.

I would also like to thank my students from the University of Portland, where I taught for sixteen years. My time there gave me the wisdom and experience that has shaped me into the writing coach and educator I am today. Teaching over a thousand undergraduates how to transform from students to writers fostered the creation of approaches to reach every kind of learner and writer. To my University of Portland colleague, Cheri Buck-Perry, with whom I shared an office and eventually started a business, I am indebted to the hours of intellectual and pedagogical conversations about learning, reading, writing, and imagination.

Additionally, I would like to give my heartfelt thanks to the writers who agreed to share their work in this book. I remember the process of working together with great fondness and follow your successes in college and beyond, as your devoted fan. Your bravery and vulnerability to create these essays and show colleges a glimpse of who you are deserves all of our admiration. Thank you for helping me show other college-bound seniors how to create standout essays and help them open doors by making a great first impression.

Finally, I want to thank the Panet-Raymond family who generously supported the inclusion of Nicole's essay in this book. I was so fortunate to have interviewed Nicole before she passed away suddenly, and I am so pleased to share Nicole's beautiful writing with the world, knowing her voice will live on and inspire others as they pursue their dreams.

ABOUT THE AUTHOR

Photo by A.J. Coots

Victoria Payne is a writer, writing coach, and the founder of Boxcar Writing Labs. For sixteen years, she taught writing at the University of Portland, receiving the Dean's Award for Excellence in Teaching for Part-Time Faculty in 2017. Her work has helped hundreds of students write about their lives with style and substance. Victoria traces her love of story back to her childhood in Georgia, where the melody of storytelling was all around her. As a writer, she believes stories are the common language we speak to each other. *Write Big* is her first book, combining her experience teaching in the university classroom, her years as a writing coach, and her profound belief that writing gives us the tools and the wisdom to discover our role as the main character in our own fascinating story. In the last decade, many college-bound seniors have used her lessons, collected in *Write Big*, to create standout application essays, gain admission into their dream schools, and strengthen their writing skills before college. Victoria lives, writes, and works in Portland, Oregon.

Made in the USA
San Bernardino, CA
27 May 2018